INTERNATIONAL DEVELOPMENT IN FOCUS

Shadows of Conflict in Northern and Eastern Sri Lanka

Socioeconomic Challenges and a Way Forward

Anna O'Donnell, Mohamed Ghani Razaak,
Markus Kostner, and Jeeva Perumpillai-Essex

WORLD BANK GROUP

Contents

Figures

Maps

Tables

Abbreviations

BPO	business process outsourcing
DS	divisional secretaries
FGD	focus group discussions
FLFP	female labor force participation
GDP	gross domestic product
HIES	Household Income Expenditure Survey
IDP	internally displaced persons
IMR	infant mortality rates
KII	key informant interviews
LA	local authorities
LTTE	Liberation Tigers of Tamil Eelam
MMR	maternal mortality rates
PGDP	provincial gross domestic products
PTSD	posttraumatic stress disorder
STEP	Skills Towards Employability and Productivity

About the Authors

Markus Kostner has over 25 years of experience in the areas of fragility and conflict, violence prevention, crisis response, and social development. He has worked extensively on Africa, Latin America, Middle East, and Southeast Asia. He has broad operational and analytical experience in the fields of demobilization and reintegration of ex-combatants, community-driven development, conflict and postconflict engagement, and postdisaster social impacts analysis. Kostner has worked at the World Bank, the Vienna University of Economics and Business, the Austrian Ministry of Foreign Affairs, and other institutions. He holds an MBA and a doctorate in economics from the Vienna University of Economics and Business.

Anna O'Donnell is a Senior Social Development Specialist in the Social, Urban, Rural and Resilience Global Practice of the World Bank in Washington, DC. Since joining the World Bank, she has worked on issues involving social resilience, community-driven development, low-income housing, and youth inclusion in the digital economy, primarily in the South Asia Region. O'Donnell holds a doctorate in sociology from the University of Maryland, where her research focused on outcomes of efficiency and equity in participatory community-based organizations.

Jeeva Perumpillai-Essex has over 35 years of experience as a Development Economist addressing issues of poverty and sustainable business in the Africa, East Asia and Pacific, and South Asia regions. Perumpillai-Essex worked at the World Bank for over twenty years, as well as at the International Finance Corporation. Since 2015, she has been living in Sri Lanka, where she is developing and advising on programs and projects in the public and private sectors on sustainable growth of the Northern Province in Sri Lanka. She has also been working with civil society groups on designing and implementing sustainable livelihood programs with a focus on women. She holds a master's degree in agriculture economics from the University of New England in Australia.

Mohamed Ghani Razaak joined the World Bank in 2010, working in the Colombo office, where he supported social development considerations in several postconflict development projects in Sri Lanka's Northern and Eastern provinces, as well urban, health, education, and community-centered development projects. Since 2016, he has been working in the Europe and Central Asia Region of the World Bank. Prior to joining the World Bank, Razaak worked as a Senior Lecturer at the Department of Sociology, Peradeniya University, Sri Lanka. In addition, he worked as a Consultant to the Asian Development Bank and the International Fund for Agriculture Development, and he published several articles and research papers on human security, forced migration, and rural development issues in Sri Lanka. Razaak holds a master's degree in development sociology from Colorado State University, and a doctorate in applied sociology from La Trobe University, Melbourne, Australia, where his research focused on internally displaced persons affected by the civil conflict in Sri Lanka.

1 Introduction

Sri Lanka has made significant strides in social and economic development over the past decade. Economic growth has averaged over seven percent a year over the past five years, following an average growth rate of six percent in the preceding five years. Sri Lanka has also made notable strides in reducing poverty and promoting shared prosperity. The national poverty headcount ratio declined from 22.7 to 6.7 percent between 2002 and 2012/13. Consumption per capita of the bottom 40 percent grew at 3.3 percent a year, compared to 2.8 percent for the total population. Human development indicators, such as educational and health outcomes, also supersede many regional and lower middle-income standards (Newhouse, Becerra, and Doan 2016).

However, these advancements mask several pockets of the country where poverty rates are high, most notably the Northern and the Eastern provinces of the country. The eight districts that make up these two provinces have some of the highest poverty rates in the country (map 1.1). Six of the eight districts in the Northern and Eastern provinces exhibit poverty rates that are above Sri Lanka's national average of 6.7 percent. In particular, the districts of Mullativu, Mannar, and Batticaloa, with poverty rates of 28.8, 20.1 and 19.4 percent, respectively, are some of the highest rates in the country. Taken together, the Northern and Eastern provinces represent some of the poorest areas of the country. More recent preliminary poverty data show that, while overall poverty has declined in Sri Lanka, the Northern and Eastern provinces continue to exhibit poverty rates of 7.7 and 7.3 percent, respectively, which is above the national average (of 4.1 percent).

OBJECTIVE OF THE SOCIOECONOMIC ASSESSMENT

The objective of the socioeconomic assessment is to gain a better understanding of the current social and economic conditions and dynamics in the Northern and Eastern provinces, with a view to better inform programmatic engagement in these two provinces. Specifically, the study looked across the districts of the

MAP 1.1

Poverty rates by district, 2012/13 HIES

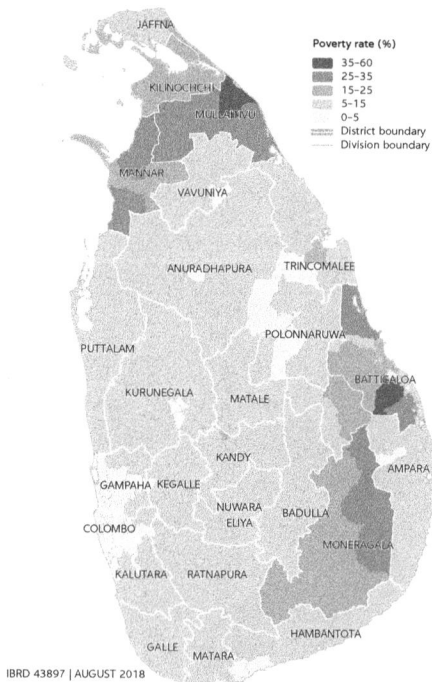

Poverty rate (%)
- 35–60
- 25–35
- 15–25
- 5–15
- 0–5
- District boundary
- Division boundary

IBRD 43897 | AUGUST 2018

	POVERTY HEAD COUNT INDEX (%)	POOR HOUSEHOLDS (%)
Sri Lanka	**6.7**	**5.3**
Northern Province	**10.9**	**8.8**
Jaffna	8.3	6.6
Mannar	20.1	15.0
Vavuniya	3.4	2.4
Mullativu	28.8	24.7
Killinochchi	12.7	10.7
Eastern Province	**11.0**	**8.0**
Batticoloa	19.4	14.3
Amapara	5.4	4.1
Trincomalee	9.0	6.2

Sources: Central Bank of Sri Lanka 2016.
Note: HIES = Household Income Expenditure Survey

North and East to determine key socioeconomic and demographic patterns, as well as labor force dynamics, and economic information. This was complemented by an in-depth analysis with social groups—both directly and indirectly affected by the conflict—with a view to better understand the postwar and current social and community dynamics of the area.

The assessment is made up of six background studies, including reports on (a) the provincial economies and economic structures of the North and East; (b) labor force dynamics; (c) demographic changes and impacts on vulnerability; (d) the psychosocial needs of the local population; (e) community and social institutions; and (f) livelihood trends and impacts of the war on productive assets. These studies were informed by both quantitative and qualitative data, as well as secondary literature identified for the purposes of this assessment. Quantitative assessments made use of "Labour Force Survey" (2011–15),[1] the "Household Income and Expenditure Survey" (2012/13), the Sri Lanka 2011 National Census (Department of Census and Statistics n.d.) Central Bank of Sri Lanka statistics, the "Annual Survey of Industries" (Department of Census and Statistics. 2015a), the "Skills Towards Employability and Productivity (STEP) Survey"[2], and an enterprise survey (2011). Qualitative data was collected in the field through Key Informant Interviews (KII), Individual Interviews (II) and Focus Group Discussions (FGDs), covering a number of topics, including mental health, livelihoods, community dynamics, gender relations, youth issues, and vulnerable populations. The findings of the work were further validated through district level stakeholder consultations in each of the eight districts in the provinces, and a national stakeholder workshop. This report provides a summary of the key findings from the assessments, as well as emerging recommendations to improve the socioeconomic conditions of the Northern and Eastern provinces.

BACKGROUND

Sri Lanka's Northern and Eastern provinces together cover around 28.1 percent of the total land area of the country, with a population of 2.8 million (14 percent of the national population). While Sri Lanka is predominantly Sinhalese, the eight districts that make up the Northern and Eastern provinces are ethnically diverse; the Northern Province is predominantly Tamil, and the Eastern Province's population is evenly divided among Tamils, Muslims and Sinhalese. The Northern and Eastern provinces today are younger, on average, than the rest of Sri Lanka. The Northern Province is predominantly rural, with only Jaffna as an urban center, whereas the Eastern Province has around one quarter of the population living in urban areas, a figure that is significantly higher than Sri Lanka's average (table 1.1). The economic base of the Northern and Eastern provinces continues to be dominated by agriculture and fisheries, though there is a growing industrial base in the Eastern Province. Contributions to the national GDP remain low, although economic growth has been over 10 percent in both provinces over the past several years.

TABLE 1.1 Selected indicators of the Northern and Eastern provinces

VARIABLE	NORTHERN PROVINCE	EASTERN PROVINCE	SRI LANKA
Area (sq. km)	8,884	9,996	65,707
Population (millions)	1.1	1.6	20.4
Population share (%)	5.2	7.6	100.0
Population density		174.5	
Age profile (% of individuals)			
<15 years	26.7	30.4	25.2
15–24 years	18.4	18.1	15.6
25–34 years	15.6	15.9	15.7
35–44 years	11.9	12.8	13.6
45–54 years	10.7	10.9	12.3
55–64 years	9.4	7.2	9.7
65+ years	7.2	4.7	7.9
Ethnicity (%)			
Sinhalese	3.0	23.2	74.9
Tamil (Sri Lankan & Indian Tamil)	93.1	39.2	11.1
Muslim	3.1	36.9	9.3
Other	0.8	0.7	4.7
Urban (%)	13.4	23.1	16.3
Years of education	8.2	7.2	8.2
Poverty (%)	10.9	11.0	6.7
Employment rate (%)	43.7	44.1	50.9

Sources: Department of Census and Statistics n.d.; Department of Census and Statistics 2014.
Note: The Labour Force Survey is conducted annually by the Department of Census and Statistics, government of Sri Lanka.

TABLE 1.2 **Phases of the Sri Lankan civil war**

NAME	YEARS COVERED	DISTRICTS AFFECTED
Eelam War I	1983–87	Jaffna, Colombo (Black July), Mullativu, Anaradhapura
Indian Peace Keeping Force	1987–90	Jaffna, Trincomalee
Eelam War II	1990–94	Jaffna, Kilinochchi, Mullativu, Mannar, Batticaloa, Trincomalee (partially)
Eelam War III	1995–2001	Kilinochchi, Mullativu, Mannar, Batticaloa, Trincomalee (partially)
Ceasefire	2001–05	
Eelam War IV	2006–09	Kilinochchi, Mullativu, Mannar
War ends in Eastern Province	July 2007	Trincomalee, Batticaloa
Last stand and defeat of LTTE	May 2009	Kilinochchi, Mullativu

Source: World Bank compilation.
Note: LTTE = Liberation Tigers of Tamil Eelam.

Sri Lanka's civil war

Sri Lanka's Northern and Eastern provinces were at the center of an armed conflict that evolved over nearly three decades, beginning in the early 1980s. Ethnic and linguistic differences combined with political, economic and ideological grievances contributed to the emergence of an armed Tamil militant formation in the beginning of the 1980s, which in turn came to be dominated by the Liberation Tigers of Tamil Eelam (LTTE). The conflict between the LTTE and the government of Sri Lanka included four phases of war (1983–87; 1990–94; 1995–2001, and 2006–09) and three failed attempts at peace building (1987–90; 1994–95; 2001–06) (de Mel and Venugopal 2016) (table 1.2). At its most expansive, the LTTE controlled around 75 percent of the territories of the Northern and Eastern provinces, with approximately 25 percent of the total population living in the LTTE controlled areas. The LTTE had a separate administration system, police force and justice system. During this time, and what perhaps makes Sri Lanka unique, is that throughout the war, the central government retained a presence in the LTTE controlled areas. This meant that over the nearly three decades of war, aside from periods of intense fighting, many health, education and other core services continued to be delivered, although with some disruption and quality issues, particularly during periods of active fighting (Mampily 2011).

Throughout the different phases of war, fighting was primarily concentrated in the Northern and Eastern provinces of the country, causing widespread destruction, displacement and subsequent economic and social consequences. However, even within these provinces, the intensity of fighting, displacement and destruction was uneven, with much of the fighting concentrated in a few districts, particularly as the Sri Lankan army stepped up its military engagement between 2007 and 2009. The war ended in 2007 in the Eastern Province, with the defection of key LTTE leaders, and in 2009, the war ended in the Northern Province after a decisive military victory by the Sri Lankan government forces.

Sri Lanka's war caused significant damage to infrastructure and service delivery. The Northern Province estimates that of its 1,958.6 km of provincial roads, and 7,600 km of rural roads, only 20–25 percent were in good condition after the conflict (Provincial Planning Secretariat 2009). The war also impacted the education sector. The Northern Province estimated that in 2009, there was a shortage of around 1,650 teachers in the province. In addition, the conflict had led to displacement and educational disruption in the province, especially in the Vanni districts.[3] The conflict had destroyed schools, roads and hospitals, as well as laboratories, libraries, administrative blocks and teacher's quarters. The health sector was also impacted, with an estimated 90 percent of vacancies in the specialist cadre and a shortage of medical officers in the province (estimated at 50 percent) (Provincial Planning Secretariat 2009). Compared to the preconflict period, maternal mortality rates (MMR) and infant mortality rates (IMR) worsened (Wanasundera 2006; Johnson 2017).

NOTES

1. The Labour Force Survey is conducted annually by the Department of Census and Statistics, government of Sri Lanka.
2. Data from the Skills Towards Employability and Productivity (STEP) Survey were from 2012.
3. These districts include Kilinochchi, Mullaitivu, and Mannar, and are the location of much of the fighting between the LTTE and government forces in 2009.

REFERENCES

Central Bank of Sri Lanka. 2016. *Economic and Social Statistics of Sri Lanka*. Government of Sri Lanka.

de Mel, N., and R. Venugopal. "Peacebuilding Context Assessment: Sri Lanka 2016," March 2016. United Nations. http://lk.one.un.org/wp-content/uploads/2016/04/Peacebuilding-Context-Assessment-Draft-1-single-pages.pdf.

Department of Census and Statistics. 2011. *Sri Lanka Labour Force Survey*. Government of Sri Lanka.

——. 2012. *Sri Lanka Labour Force Survey*. Government of Sri Lanka.

——. 2013a. *Household Income and Expenditure Survey 2012/13*. Government of Sri Lanka.

——. 2013b. *Sri Lanka Labour Force Survey*. Government of Sri Lanka.

——. 2014. *Sri Lanka Labour Force Survey*. Government of Sri Lanka.

——. 2015a. *Annual Survey of Industries*. Government of Sri Lanka.

——. 2015b. *Sri Lanka Labour Force Survey*. Government of Sri Lanka.

——. n.d. "Census of Population and Housing 2011." Government of Sri Lanka.

Johnson, S. 2017. "The Cost of War on Public Health: An Exploratory Method for Understanding the Impact of Conflict on Public Health in Sri Lanka." *PLoS One* 12 (1): 1–28.

Mampily, Z. 2011. *Rebel Rulers: Insurgent Governance and Civilian Life during War*. Ithaca, New York: Cornell University Press.

Newhouse, David Locke, Pablo Suarez Becerra, and Dung Doan. 2016. *Sri Lanka Poverty and Welfare: Recent Progress and Remaining Challenges*. Washington, DC: World Bank.

Provincial Planning Secretariat. 2009. "Five Year Investment Programme: 2009–2013." Northern Provincial Council. https://www.np.gov.lk/pdf/publications/5_year_programme.pdf.

Wanasundera, L. 2006. *Rural Women in Sri Lanka's Post-Conflict Rural Economy*. Bangkok, Thailand: Food and Agriculture Organization of the United Nations, RAP Publication 2006/13. http://www.fao.org/3/a-ag114e.pdf.

2 Economic and Social Developments in the Northern and Eastern Provinces during the Conflict

The current dynamics and economic structure of the Northern and Eastern province exhibit characteristics of postconflict growth; high rates of economic growth are taking place against a low base, as peace and stability are returning. In order to understand the current dynamics of the Northern and Eastern provinces, it is important to highlight the impacts of the war on the economic and social structure of these areas. During the war, the destruction of critical infrastructure, assets, and the displacement of people contributed to a decline in economic production, particularly in the agricultural and fisheries sector. This decline in economic production was further exacerbated by an economic embargo imposed from 1990 to 2001, and again from 2005 to 2009, further eroding competitiveness. Widespread displacement and an emerging male deficit further affected the labor force of the Northern and Eastern provinces, leading to the collapse of agriculture and the emergence of daily wage labor. These impacts continue to affect the development of the region today.

BACKGROUND

Sri Lanka began pursuing a program of economic liberalization in 1977, opening the country to foreign capital and relaxing import restrictions, placing a greater emphasis on private enterprise, and focusing on an export-led strategy of growth. Trade and exchange controls were liberalized, and a new economic policy, dependent on private investment and market forces, was introduced (Gamage 2009). New policies also ushered in several changes to the governance system, further centralizing the governance structure of the country under an executive president (Gamage 2009). With liberalization, Sri Lanka's economy moved from a predominantly agrarian and service economy, to a service economy today. With this, the share of the agricultural sector in gross domestic product (GDP) went from 30 percent in the 1970s to only 8 percent in 2014. Today, the services sector dominates the Sri Lankan economy, with over half (56.7 percent) of GDP coming from this sector in 2014.

With the outbreak of war in 1983, the Northern and Eastern provinces saw fighting, destruction and economic decline, which particularly affected the backbone of the provincial economies: the agriculture sector. The Northern and Eastern provinces are in Sri Lanka's dry zone, which produces paddy and coconut. In 1980, the production of paddy, vegetables, chilies, tobacco, dairy products, fish products and fruits were substantial in the Northern Province, and the province contributed around 10 percent of national paddy production and 20 percent of national fish production. There were also light engineering, apparel manufacturing and other small industrial establishments (Samaratunga 2010). The Eastern Province also produced a significant amount of paddy, relying on an ancient and well-established irrigation system (Samaratunga 2010). By the end of the war, the Northern Province contributed less than 3 percent to agricultural production and fisheries had declined to 10–12 percent of national production.[1,2] In 2009, contributions to national GDP were some of the lowest in the country, at 3.3 and 5.8 percent for the Northern and Eastern provinces, respectively.

It is difficult to know what would have happened to agricultural production in the Northern and Eastern provinces in the absence of war. Economic liberalization brought in export oriented growth, and Sri Lanka's economy shifted to manufacturing, and eventually to services over this period. Changes in global trade patterns and communication technologies also may have affected the competitiveness of the sector within domestic and international markets. However, it is impossible to discount the impact of the war, both on the sector and the labor force. Specifically, the war caused the destruction of critical rural infrastructure, widespread displacement, and changes in land use that all contributed to the relative decline of the sector. While Sri Lanka's economy shifted to manufacturing and eventually services, these sectors were constrained by the war as well. Thus, the economic impacts of the war on the Northern and Eastern provinces cannot be underestimated, and are a critical component for understanding postwar growth and development challenges.

ECONOMIC IMPACT OF THE CONFLICT

The impact of Sri Lanka's civil war on the Northern and Eastern provincial economies are twofold. First, the destruction of infrastructure—including roads, markets, water and power supply stations, and irrigation tanks—led to the breakdown of agricultural production, local markets and productive organizations, and stifled industry and growth of the private sector. Displacement and restrictions effectively halved production in the fisheries sector. Industrial production was hampered by poor transportation networks, instability, and lack of reliable access to power and water. Under the uncertainties of war, the private sector left, along with significant capital and employment opportunities. These impacts affected economic growth and productivity over the war period, from which the Northern and Eastern provinces are now slowly emerging.

Second, the economic impacts were further exacerbated by an embargo put in place from 1999 to 2001, and then again from 2005 to 2009, which severely limited the movement of goods, services and people—especially through the districts of Kilinochchi, Mannar, Mullaitivu and parts of Vavuniya. This included restrictions on inputs such as fertilizer for agriculture, as well as cement (Rajah 2017). This led to a decline in agricultural production in the area, and essentially created a closed production system within the Liberation Tigers of Tamil Eelam (LTTE) controlled area, affecting much of the local population and livelihoods. The embargo also further stifled local industry and the private sector, ultimately leading to a near collapse of production in both sectors. In addition, goods and services became more expensive for the local population and less widely available. While Jaffna was not under LTTE control at the time, the embargo also impacted the Jaffna peninsula, as transportation to the district was difficult (World Bank 2009). The two main segments of the economy—agriculture and fisheries—were negatively affected by the embargo, and especially after 1990 there was a marked decline in production (Sarvananthan 2007).

Agriculture sector

The agriculture sector—including agriculture, livestock and fisheries—constituted the largest employer for much of the Northern and Eastern province prior to the war, particularly for the rural population.[3] During the war, agricultural production declined because of a combination of displacement, increasing salinity, the establishment of high security zones, damage to irrigation infrastructure, land mines, lack of access to markets and lack of capital (Wanasundera 2006). The destruction of roads and markets disrupted local economies, led to the breakdown of private-sector input and output markets and technical support services, diminished input supply and extension services for farm and nonfarm produce, and diluted cooperatives and other productive organizations. The relationship between agricultural production and the war can easily be seen in production capabilities during ceasefire periods; paddy acreage increased by 7 percent during the ceasefire agreement of 2002–05, demonstrating an inverse relationship between production and war (figure 2.1).

FIGURE 2.1

Paddy production by province, 1979–2015

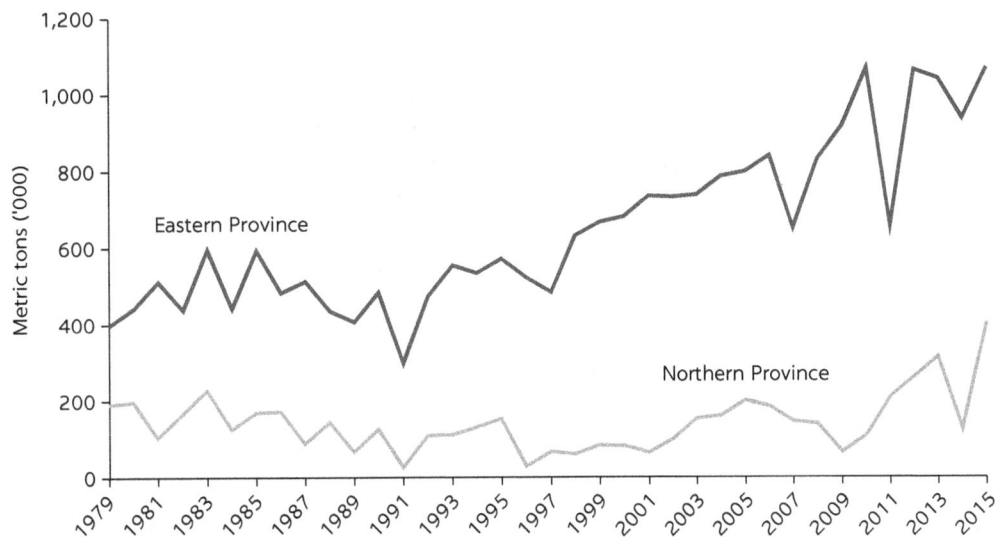

Source: Agriculture and Environment Statistic Division, Department of Census and Statistics, Sri Lanka.

The destruction of critical infrastructure led to overall declines in production that would remain lower than preconflict output through the end of the war. It is estimated that in 1990, the fisheries sector accounted for 35 percent of the agriculture sector in the Northern Province. However, over the next five years, the sector collapsed because of reduced mobility, a ban on motorized boats, the destruction of fishing gear and assets, and disrupted marketing links, leading to a 12 percent negative growth rate (Wanasundera 2006). Reduced restrictions in offshore fishing led to the growth of the fisheries sector after 2002, and then again after 2009 (Wanasundera 2006). Collapse of the agriculture sector during the conflict further impoverished rural households. IDPs seeking to recommence farming were constrained by a lack of inputs and access to markets, and many continue to engage in subsistence level farming and small-scale economic activities (Wanasundera 2006).

Agricultural land

Alongside the decline in agricultural production, significant land use changes also occurred over the 26 years of war. Decline in agricultural land and concomitant increases in nonagricultural land uses were caused by a series of drivers, including the deterioration of operation and maintenance of irrigation systems for agricultural water supply, the unavailability of fuel and other production inputs, difficulty harvesting and transporting produce, and the imposition of security forces in some of the high potential agricultural lands. Widespread use of landmines further affected the use of agricultural lands (Hemapala 2006). Such disruptions to conventional agricultural systems left poor and marginalized farmer communities in villages, which were already affected by fighting between armed groups and security forces, less capable to cope with hazards of the natural environment (Sudhakar and Bui 2008).

Asian tsunami

The decline, especially of the agriculture and fisheries sectors, was further exacerbated by the Asian tsunami which made landfall on December 26, 2004.[4] Given the eroded competitiveness of the sector, the tsunami affected resource based livelihoods in the agriculture sector, destroying inputs, crops, livestock and fisheries. The geographic impact of the tsunami was uneven, with much of the coastal belt of the Northern, Eastern, and Southern provinces, and some parts of the Western Province severely damaged. The coastal areas in the districts of Ampara, Batticaloa, Trincomalee, Kilinochchi, Mullaitivu, and Jaffna were seriously affected, accounting for two-thirds of deaths and almost 60 per cent of the resulting displacement. The severity of the tsunami disaster in the Northern and Eastern provinces compounded problems arising from the conflict: the majority of the 360,000 internally displaced people lived in these two provinces at the time of the tsunami, and the disaster caused damage and destruction to the marginalized and poorer populations involved in natural resource dependent livelihoods (i.e., agriculture and fisheries). Around 50 percent of the homes destroyed were in the Eastern Province, and 11 percent were in the Northern Province. Relief efforts in both provinces were also affected by the ongoing conflict, and by the lack of access for post-tsunami rehabilitation work. In the aftermath of the tsunami, relief and humanitarian support brought an inflow of assistance that temporarily boosted the local economy.

Industry

While the Northern and Eastern provinces were not industrial hubs, prior to the war, large- and medium-scale industries existed, including cement, paper, and seafood processing, as well as small-scale industries (Northern Provincial Council 2017). Declines in the industry sector were due to damaged infrastructure, lost equipment, disruption to service delivery and production, the displacement of labor, and poor access to markets. While figures vary, some estimates indicate that around 752 industries were active in the Northern Province prior to the war. In the Eastern Province, manufacturing grew during the war period, primarily in areas that were less affected by active fighting from 1999 onwards, and by 2005, Trincomalee District was a major contributor to manufacturing output in the Eastern Province.

Services

The services sector has grown to dominate Sri Lanka's economy, with contributions from dynamic private enterprises in wholesale and retail trade, communications and transportation and finance (Central Bank of Sri Lanka 2016). However, similar patterns of strong private-sector growth are not mirrored in the war affected Northern and Eastern provinces. Estimates in 2005 show that while the services sector had grown to almost half of the provincial economies, much of this was from lower value addition sub-sectors. In 2005, contributions from transportation and communications, wholesale and retail trade and banking totaled 19.3 and 20 percent in the Northern and Eastern provinces, respectively. The largest share of the services subsector came from public administration and defense (38 percent in the Northern Province and 11 percent in the Eastern Province, as compared to only 5 percent of Sri Lanka's GDP) (Sarvananthan 2007). These figures are reflective of the diminished role of the private sector in the conflict region, as well as the relief and redevelopment functions of the public sector (Sarvananthan 2007).

Overall labor and employment

Impacts on economic production resulted in a shortage of employment opportunities and widespread vulnerability and social and economic insecurity during the war that continue to today. In the Northern and Eastern provinces, during the war period, statistics show a shift among the employed population from agriculture to industry, and a slight increase in services. However, labor force participation was low, estimated at 36 and 46 percent in the Northern and Eastern provinces, respectively, both well below the national average of 49 percent (2004) (Samaratunga 2010). Some studies estimate that labor shifted from the formal to the informal sector, with a growth in daily wage labor, particularly among displaced populations (Wanasundera 2006; see also Silva 2018). Thus, by 2004, the economies of the Northern and Eastern provinces were demonstrating severe underemployment and low labor productivity in several sectors of the economy, with predominant employment in agriculture, where low levels of productivity were also observed (Sarvananthan 2007).

SOCIAL IMPACTS OF THE CONFLICT

Sri Lanka's civil war had demographic impacts on the population that affect local economic production and livelihoods, as well as social structures and relations. The war period was associated with deaths, both civilian and military, as well as forced and voluntary conscription. The conflict also contributed to large-scale population shifts and movements, leading to a disruption of the social fabric and the erosion of community institutions. While no official figures exist, it is estimated that, over 26 years of conflict, more than 100,000 people of all ethnicities lost their lives, and hundreds of thousands were injured. The conflict also caused significant internal and external displacement, estimated at around 800,000 people at its peak in 2001. It is currently estimated that around 90,000 people (0.4 percent of the total population) are internally displaced in Sri Lanka, and an estimated 100,000 refugees continue to live in the southern Indian state of Tamil Nadu (Siriwardhana and Wickramage 2014). In addition, there is a large diaspora population (numbering nearly 1 million) in North America, Europe, and Australia, which migrated during the war years.

Periods of active fighting also led to a brain drain, capital flight, outmigration, and multiple displacements that affected the local socioeconomic context in several ways. The phases of migration and displacement saw the relatively affluent leave first, leading to brain drain and capital flight, loss of industries and businesses, and an economic downturn in the area. Second, populations facing multiple displacement over generations were exposed to shocks and trauma throughout periods of living in camps for internally displaced persons (IDPs) or while being displaced from their homes. While most households have been resettled, the psychosocial challenges of their ordeal remain, and assets have to be rebuilt. Finally, those unable to migrate were typically the worst off, without economic or social capital or networks to flee the war, and remained on the frontlines where they witnessed combat, death, and associated trauma. Today, not only do these populations remain poor and marginalized, as many of their assets were destroyed, but they also face a higher incidence of trauma as compared to all other groups. Taken together, the massive population movements, both out of the Northern and Eastern provinces during the war, as well as population movements back into these areas since the end of the war, have contributed to an erosion of community support structures, networks and the overall social fabric that are still only in the nascent stages of being rebuilt today.

Displacement and migration

The armed conflict in Sri Lanka led to the displacement of populations and outmigration from the Northern and Eastern provinces (figure 2.2). The table below shows only those internally displaced in Sri Lanka, by district, between 1983 and 2009 (table 2.1). This does not include those who migrated out of the country.

The displacement and migration that took place in the Northern and Eastern provinces followed specific patterns, with the relatively affluent and skilled labor leaving first, followed by the middle class and finally the relatively poor. In the early phases of the war, migrants from the Jaffna district arguably followed an established pattern of the outmigration of males for work

FIGURE 2.2

Trends of internal displacement in Sri Lanka, 1983–2009

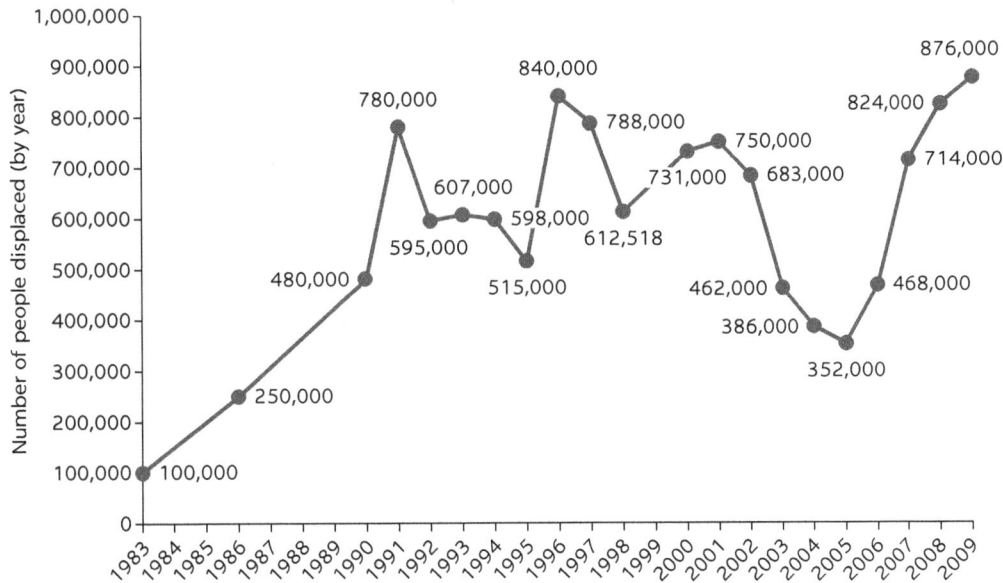

Source: Razaak (unpublished).

TABLE 2.1 **Internally displaced people in Sri Lanka, 1983–2009**

YEAR	NO. OF IDPS	DISTRICTS AFFECTED
1983	100,000	All parts of Sri Lanka
1987	250,000	Jaffna
1990	377,000	Mannar, Vavuniya, Mullaitivu, and parts of Kilinochchi (Vanni districts); and Jaffna
1991	460,000	Vanni districts and Jaffna
1992	595,000	Border villages of North and East
1998	612,518	Vanni districts
2000	731,000	Vanni districts and parts of Eastern districts
2001	788,000	Jaffna
2002	462,000	Resettlements in the North
2003	386,000	Resettlements in the North and East
2004	352,000	Resettlements in the North and East
2006	468,000	Batticaloa, Ampara, and Trinco (East)
2007	714,000	Vanni districts, Jaffna, and the East
2008	824,000	Vanni (esp. Mullaithivu, Kilinochchi)
2009 December	876,000	Vanni (Mullaithivu, Kilinochchi)

Sources: These data were drawn from the following as quoted in Razaak (unpublished): Internal Displacement Monitoring Centre, United Nations High Commission for Refugees, and Ministry of Resettlement and Rehabilitation of Sri Lanka; and Acharya 2007.
Note: IDP = internally displaced persons.

and better economic opportunities—a pattern well established from the colonial era onwards (Pfaffenberger 1982; Silva 2017). Thus, early migrants from the conflict were able to utilize social networks and capital. Many of the early migrants were engaged in highly skilled employment, including commercialized agriculture, business, and private enterprise (Silva 2017).

The second wave of migrants were those who fled to avoid capture, cross-fire, death, advancing troops, or simply out of the fear of being killed. Many of these households also faced economic hardship and food shortages created by the fighting, or were forcibly expelled by the LTTE or security forces. Most of the households impacted by this displacement were from the Northern and Eastern provinces, with around 80 percent of the IDPs concentrated in the Northern Province, particularly in the southern most district of Vavuniya (Razaak unpublished). At the end of 2009, half of those displaced were in government supported welfare centers and camps, with another one third living with relatives and friends, or in rented houses of their own outside the war zone (Ministry of Economic Development 2010). Most of the IDPs were Tamils (84 percent), with Muslims and Sinhalese accounting for 11 and 4 percent, respectively, of the total number of IDPs.[5]

Patterns of displacement over the duration of Sri Lanka's civil war have contributed to eroding community and family structures, as well as weakened social networks and social capital. Three kinds of displacement took place because of the war: first, conflict-induced internal displacement that results in the long-term or protracted displacement of households; second, short term displacement; and finally, those who experience multiple incidences of displacement. Households experiencing multiple incidences of displacement are the worst off, having repeatedly lost assets, property, livelihoods and family members. The majority of those who were displaced multiple times were also Tamils who directly experienced the impacts of the war (Razaak unpublished).

Demographic impacts

The war also had a demographic impact on the population of the Northern and Eastern provinces. In general, the war and related causalities and population movements, combined with a markedly higher life expectancy among women, have led to a slightly unbalanced sex ratio among all ethnic groups. However, when considering demographic data at the provincial, or even the district level, the sex ratios within the populations do not seem to differ significantly from the rest of the country.

Disaggregation by age group and ethnicity revealed certain patterns of a male deficit, especially in the economically active labor force, rather than among economically dependent children and the elderly. This has corresponding implications for the earning capacity of households, social welfare, the structure of the family, security, psychosocial developments, political participation and gender relations in society more broadly. Changes in the sex ratio are also most evident among the Sri Lankan Tamils, who comprise the largest single ethnic group in the Northern and Eastern provinces. The resident Sri Lankan Tamil population in the Northern Province, and that of the Jaffna District, in particular, are characterized by a significant male deficit (figure 2.3).

This skewed sex ratio continues to have several secondary impacts on labor force dynamics in the Northern and Eastern provinces. First, the specific patterns of male deficit in the Northern and Eastern provinces have influenced the structure of the labor force. Of the two main rural livelihoods—agriculture and fishing—there are specific gendered roles for men and women in cultivation, processing, and fishing activities (Sireeranhan 2013). With the loss of working age males during the war period, combined with destruction of critical rural infrastructure and restrictions on markets, the agricultural and fisheries

FIGURE 2.3

Age-specific sex ratios in the Jaffna District, 2011

Age-sex distribution of population in Jaffna District

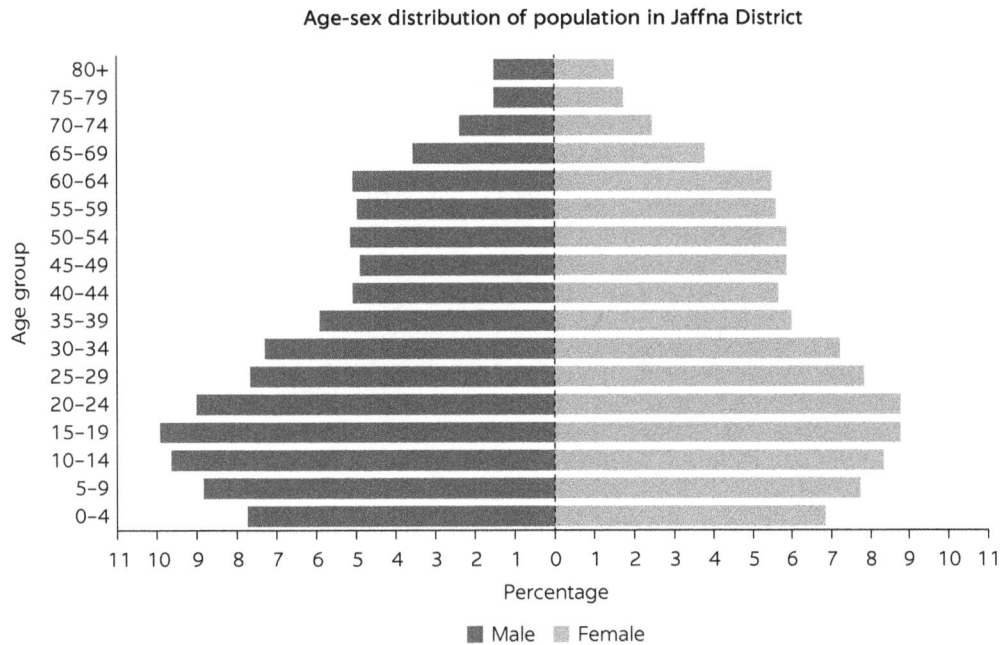

Source: Sri Lanka Census of Population and Housing 2011 n.d.

cooperatives once active in the Northern and Eastern provinces collapsed, and production dropped. There is some evidence to show that, in the absence of males, women's roles in agriculture and fishing had expanded beyond traditional gendered roles during the war, with more women engaging in traditionally male dominated roles in agriculture, such as fishing, fish processing, marketing, net making and net repair (Wanasundera 2006). However, wage differentials persisted throughout this period, with women typically earning half of what men made for similar labor, and a lack of available labor contributed to the overall collapse of the sectors.

With the breakdown of agriculture, fisheries and industries, many households in the Northern and Eastern provinces turned to daily wage labor as the dominant livelihood strategy, particularly for the poorer segments of the population (Jayatilaka, Amirthalingam, and Gunasekara 2015; Razaak 2014; Sarvananthan, Jeyapraba, and Alagarajah 2017; Silva, Sivakanthan, and Wickramasinghe 2012). Some studies have estimated that wage labor was the primary livelihood for over 75 percent of households in the war-affected Northern and Eastern regions. In part due to the oversupply of unskilled female workers in the informal sector, which in turn was an outcome of the unbalanced sex ratio described in the preceding section, the daily wage of an unskilled female worker was usually less than 50 percent of the daily wage given to an unskilled male worker. Collapse of the agriculture sector during the conflict further impoverished rural households. Hence, as previously noted, for those IDPs who sought to reengage in farming, such endeavors were stifled by a lack of inputs and access to markets, leading many to remain in substance level farming and other small-scale economic activities (Wanasundera 2006).

The skewed sex ratio also affects the vulnerability of women in the Northern and Eastern provinces. While gender imbalances during war periods can often dilute norms and customary restrictions on women's behavior and movement, they can also serve to limit women's roles even further. Evidence from studies during the war in Sri Lanka suggest that restrictive gender norms for women were exacerbated. Specifically, physical mobility was restricted because of security concerns, support systems collapsed because of displacement and migration, and physical and psychological abuse within the home increased because of growing alcohol consumption. In addition, the conflict reinforced the practice of early marriage in the North and East (primarily as a strategy to provide security to young girls, and to avoid recruitment) (Wanasundera 2006). Although necessity may expand women's agency during a conflict, as combatants, sole providers of a household, or even peace negotiators, the end of a conflict often restores preconflict gender norms, pushing women back to a state of disempowerment (Vithanagama 2016).

CONCLUSION

Sri Lanka's war spanned nearly three decades, and caused widespread damage to infrastructure and economic production. While the war took place against a backdrop of changes to Sri Lanka's economy, it specifically led to certain impacts that affect the economic base of the Northern and the Eastern provinces today. First, the widespread destruction of critical infrastructure, exacerbated by an economic embargo, led to a virtual collapse of the agriculture sector and constrained the growth of industry and the private sector more broadly. Displacement and an emerging gender imbalance affected the local labor supply, and further compounded the economic decline of the two provinces. The economic and social impacts of the war are relevant to further discussion on shifting priorities for growth and development today.

NOTES

1. In the Eastern Province, much of the paddy production is concentrated in Ampara and Batticaloa. The conflict did not impact this sector as much as in the Northern Province, and marginal improvements in production were seen even during the conflict period (production remained relatively unchanged at around 20 percent of national production) See Gnangasegar and Norbert (2010) and Samaratunga (2010).
2. It is also important to note the impact of the Asian tsunami which made landfall on December 26, 2004, causing widespread destruction to the coastal districts. This is described in further detail later in the document.
3. Even today, most of the districts are predominantly rural, with anywhere between 70–100 percent of the district's population residing in rural areas.
4. On December 26, 2004, the Asian tsunami made landfall in Sri Lanka, leaving 30,000 people dead, over a million people displaced, and disrupting the livelihoods of over an estimated 150,000 households. The tsunami also caused extensive damage to infrastructure and capital assets, estimated at around US$1 billion (4.5 percent of GDP), which particularly affected the tourism and fisheries sector (United Nations Needs Assessment 2005).
5. The remaining one percent of IDPs are assumed to belong to other groups. These data came from Silva 2004, as quoted in Razaak (unpublished).

REFERENCES

Acharya, Arun Kumar. 2007. "Ethnic Conflict and Refugees in Sri Lanka." *Revista De Antropogia Experimental* 7 (9): 107–21.

Central Bank of Sri Lanka. 2016. *Economic and Social Statistics of Sri Lanka*. Government of Sri Lanka.

Department of Census and Statistics. n.d. "Census of Population and Housing 2011." Government of Sri Lanka.

Gamage, S. 2009. "Economic Liberalisation, Changes in Governance Structure and Ethnic Conflict in Sri Lanka." *Journal of Contemporary Asia* 39 (2): 247–61.

Gnangasegar, R., and S. A. Norbert. 2010. "Assessment of the Impact of Cultivation of Abadoned Paddy Lands in Eastern Province." University of Colombo. http://archive.cmb.ac.lk:8080 /research/bitstream/70130/4191/1/Prof.S.A.Norbert-060.pdf.

Hemapala, K. 2006. "Effects of Landmines on Sri Lanka." *Journal of Mine Action* (Winter) (accessed August 2, 2017), https://www.jmu.edu/cisr/journal/10.2/notes/hemapala /hemapala.shtml.

Jayatilaka, D., K. Amirthalingam, and S. Gunasekara. 2015. "Conflict, Displacement and Post-War Recovery: A Community Profile of Passaiyoor East, Sri Lanka." Working Paper No. 7, Colombo: International Centre for Ethnic Studies.

Ministry of Economic Development, Sri Lanka. 2010. *Social Impact Assessment Report on the North East Local Services Improvement Project*. Colombo: NELSIP.

Northern Provincial Council. 2017. Statistical Information 2017. Northern Provincial Council. Government of Sri Lanka. http://np.gov.lk/pdf/publications/Statistical_Information _NPC_2017.pdf.

Pfaffenberger, B. 1982. *Caste in Tamil Culture: the Religious Foundation of Sudra Domination in Tamil Sri Lanka*. Syracuse: Syracuse University Press.

Rajah, A. 2017. *Government and Politics in Sri Lanka: Biopolitics and Security*. New York: Routledge Studies in South Asia Politics.

Razaak, M. Unpublished. "A Home Away from Home: Protracted Displacement of Muslims Affected by Civil War in Sri Lanka." A thesis submitted in total fulfillment of the requirements for the degree of Doctor of Philosophy, School of Social Sciences, Faculty of Humanities and Social Sciences, La Trobe University, Melbourne, Australia.

Razaak, M.G. 2014. "Living Displaced: Post-displacement Livelihood Strategies of Displaced Persons in Sri Lanka." In *Lose to Gain: Is Involuntary Resettlement a Development Opportunity?* edited by J. Perera, 58–81. Manila: Asian Development Bank.

Samaratunga, R. H. S. 2010. "Problems in Regional Development in the Northern and Eastern Provinces of Sri Lanka." http://dl.nsf.ac.lk/bitstream/handle/1/14263/ER-36%287 -8%29_34.pdf?sequence=2&isAllowed=y.

Sarvananthan, M. 2007. "Economy of the Conflict Region in Sri Lanka: From Embargo to Repression." Policy Studies 44, East-West Center. www.eastwestcenter.org/policystudies.

Sarvananthan, M., J. Suresh, and A. Alagarajah. 2017. "Feminism, Nationalism, and Labour in Post-Civil War Northern Province of Sri Lanka," Development in Practice, 27 (1): 122–128.

Silva, A. 2004. "The IDPs as Heuristic Category for Health and Social Planning in the North and East of Sri Lanka." In *National Conference of Opportunities and Challenges of the Development of Conflict Affected North-East Sri Lanka*. Peradeniya University, Sri Lanka.

Silva, K.T., S. Sivakanthan, and W.M.K.B. Wickramasinghe. 2012. "Report on Community Consultations on Underlying Causes of Poverty in Selected Conflict-Affected Areas in Sri Lanka." CARE International, Colombo.

Silva, T. 2018. "Sex Ratio and Vulnerability in Northern and Eastern Provinces in Sri Lanka." Background Paper 3, Socio-Economic Assessment of the Northern and Eastern Provinces, International Centre for Ethnic Studies, Colombo.

Sireeranhan, A. 2013. "Participation of Family-Women in Agricultural Production: A Case Study of Jaffna District, Sri Lanka." *Journal of Economics and Sustainable Development* 4 (13): 143–147.

Siriwardhana, C., and K. Wickramage. 2014. "Conflict, Forced Displacement and Health in Sri Lanka: A Review of the Research Landscape." *Conflict and Health* 8: 22.

Sudhakar, K., and E. Bui. 2008. "Land Use/Cover Changes in the War-Ravaged Jaffna Peninsula, Sri Lanka, 1984–Early 2004 in Singapore." *Journal of Tropical Geography* 29 (2).

Vithanagama, R. 2016. *Women's Economic Empowerment: A Literature Review*. Colombo: International Centre for Ethnic Studies.

Wanasundera, L. 2006. "Rural Women in Sri Lanka's Post-Conflict Rural Economy." Centre for Women's Research Sri Lanka, Food and Agriculture Organization of the United Nations, Regional Office for Asia and the Pacific, Bangkok, Thailand. RAP Publication 2006/13.

World Bank. 2009. "Reshaping Economic Geography: Sri Lanka." World Bank, Washington, DC.

3 Development Efforts in Sri Lanka's Postwar Period

Since the end of the civil war, the government of Sri Lanka initiated massive development programs in the Northern and Eastern provinces, with the objectives of resettlement, the restoration of critical infrastructure and livelihoods, and extending a range of social services to the local population. This has led to significant improvements in many areas, including the end of large-scale violence, the return of internally displaced persons (IDPs), de-mining, the construction of infrastructure, and the expansion of agriculture and fishing livelihoods (de Mel and Venugopal 2016). Two flagship government programs, one in the Eastern Province (Neganahira Navodaya), and another in the Northern Province (Uthuru Wasanthaya) are noteworthy to mention alongside several sectoral investments that also covered the Northern and Eastern provinces. Much of the focus to date has been on recovery and rehabilitation efforts in the Northern and Eastern provinces. With almost a decade elapsed since the end of the civil war, a renewed focus on the Northern and Eastern provinces will need to promote a transition from recovery to local development.

PUBLIC INVESTMENT IN THE NORTHERN AND EASTERN PROVINCES

With the end of the armed conflict in the Eastern Province in 2007, the government launched a massive investment program, entitled "Reawakening of the East" (Negenahira Navodaya). This program, initiated in July 2007, focused on improving infrastructure such as electricity, water, housing and roads in three districts of the Eastern Province and border villages (Monaragala, Badulla and Polonnaruwa). By 2009, with the end of the civil war in the Northern Province, the government launched a similar program, entitled the "Northern Spring" (Uthuru Wasanthaya). Given the large-scale displacement in the Northern Province, the Uthuru Wasanthaya program placed more emphasis on the resettlement of IDPs, the revitalization of productive sectors, the improvement of economic infrastructure, strengthening social infrastructure and fostering social services, the development of human settlements, and rebuilding the capacity of public institutions in the province. Principal among these efforts are the improvement of existing roads and the development of new road networks and bridges, restoration of the vital rail link with the Jaffna peninsula, and access to the national electrical grid and telecommunications.

Both of these national level efforts were further supported by funds from development partners, donors, and United Nations (UN) agencies. According to a report by the Ministry of Economic Development (2012), the government had set aside LKR. 425 billion for reconstruction activities in the Northern and Eastern provinces, from 2006 to 2011. For the Eastern Province alone, an estimated LKR. 199 billion was allocated, and an estimated sum of LKR. 53 billion was expended for development activities during the period from 2008 to 2011. For the Northern Province, an allocation of LKR. 244 billion was allocated for the period from 2009 to 2012 (Kay 2015).

Apart from these two major initiatives, the government also invested in the Northern and Eastern provinces through programs and projects targeting specific communities and sectors. Some of the main interventions include providing relief for displaced populations, cash grants and shelter materials for housing, efforts to restore livelihoods (particularly in agriculture, home gardening, dairy farming and livestock), and the reconstruction of critical infrastructure, including schools, hospitals and the re-establishment of administrative mechanisms (Asian Development Bank, Deutsche Gesellschaft fuer Internationale Zusammenarbeit 2015). The table below presents a summary of government expenditures in the Northern and Eastern provinces by sector or theme (table 3.1).

INVESTMENTS BY DONORS OR DEVELOPMENT PARTNERS

Development partners have also made a consistent effort in implementing programs in the North and East. Investments have generally focused on improving living conditions in the region through infrastructure development, the resettlement of IDPs, livelihood restoration, institutional development and social support. In the aftermath of the Asian tsunami, there was a sharp increase in donor expenditures in these provinces to address the impacts of the natural disaster. Much of the postdisaster relief funding was available through 2011 or 2012.

Support from development partners toward the government programs also contributed to the completion of critical infrastructure. The A9 highway, completed in December 2014, restored critical linkages between Colombo and Jaffna, and was constructed with international financing. Road networks were restored, irrigation facilities repaired, and community restoration efforts were carried out. Small scale investments in livelihood restoration were essential to the immediate income generation of the war affected populations. A large-scale housing program was supported with assistance from several donor and development agencies, which was essential for providing shelter to the nearly 250,000 displaced persons. Donor efforts were also essential for clearing 1,319 of 1,419 hazardous areas for the resettlement of individuals in their original homes (Asian Development Bank, Deutsche Gesellschaft fuer Internationale Zusammenarbeit 2015).

The estimated total amount of investments on the part of development partners in the Northern and Eastern provinces since 2009, is around US$3.4 billion.[1]

TABLE 3.1 **Estimated government expenditure in the Northern and Eastern provinces, 2009–18**

SECTOR/SUBSECTOR	AMOUNT IN US$ (MILLIONS)	AMOUNT IN LKR (MILLIONS)
Economic infrastructure	**3,344.9**	**427,245.0**
Roads	1,014.1	128,897.4
Water supply and sanitation	325.7	44,395.9
Irrigation	129.4	16.746.0
Housing	465.0	59,061.8
Fisheries	129.1	16,592.9
Electricity	83.3	10,385.6
Economic infrastructure (amounts not broken into subsectors)	664.9	83,824.5
Varied development subsectors (reconstruction & rehab.)	265.4	32,576.5
Telecommunication	0.0	0.0
Ports	0.0	0.0
Agriculture	125.3	15,578.7
Institutional and community development	103.0	14,092.4
Livestock	12.0	1,526.1
Industries	27.7	3,567.3
Social infrastructure	**407.1**	**54,396.5**
Healthcare	113.0	14,891.5
Education	160.4	22,018.9
Skills development, vocational and technical education	15.8	2,102.6
Social infrastructure (amounts not broken into subsectors)	87.2	11,381.9
(Democracy, good governance, reconciliation, human rights, Social Security Samurdhi, etc.)	25.6	3,338.8
Sports, social welfare, religious, and cultural	3.6	468.8
Women- and gender-based violence	1.5	194.0
Psychosocial support	3.6	0.0
Livelihood assistance		
Relief and livelihood assistance	67.1	8,926.6
Total	**3,819.1**	**490,568.2**

Source: World Bank compilation.
Notes: Compiled through secondary sources, including information collected from the Ministry of Finance (Budget Department); Ministry of Fisheries; Ministry of Agriculture; Ministry of Resettlement, Prison Reform, and Hindu Affairs; Ministry of National Integration and Reconciliation; Ministry of National Languages and Coexistence; Office of National Unity and Reconciliation; Ministry of Industries and Commerce; Ministry of City Planning and Water Supply; Ministry of Women's and Child Affairs; Ministry of Social Empowerment and Welfare; Ministry of Housing and Construction; as well as information received from all District Secretariats in the Northern and Eastern provinces (Jaffna, Kilinochchi, Mullaitivu, Mannar, Vavuniya, Trincomalee, Batticaloa, and Ampara), and from the Northern Provincial Council and the Eastern Provincial Council. LKR = Sri Lankan Rupees.

GAPS AND LIMITATIONS OF POSTCONFLICT DEVELOPMENT

Investments in the Northern and Eastern provinces to date have been essential to the recovery of the Northern and Eastern provinces. Various programs since 2009 have successfully resettled 887,400 people,[2] repaired 990 schools in the Northern Province, and invested in assistance to restore agriculture and fishing, two key livelihoods for the provinces. An estimated 90 percent of abandoned rice lands were cleared of mines and agriculture inputs were provided to households (Asian Development Bank, Deutsche Gesellschaft fuer

Internationale Zusammenarbeit 2015). Impact assessments of the programs show that rapid de-mining programs, new housing projects, the effective resettlement of thousands of IDPs, and large-scale infrastructure projects with a special emphasis on the North- and East-supported development efforts and wellbeing of the local populations, both direct and indirect, for the local populations.

Despite these efforts, three main gaps remain. First, the main challenge to date is the lack of available funds against recovery needs. With an estimated US\$7 billion[3] invested so far against a total estimated cost of the destruction at US\$200 billion, there are still large-scale infrastructure investment needs, particularly with regard to interior roads, transportation and communication networks, local production facilities and markets. Approximately 13,161 households are awaiting resettlement (Annual Update on Resettlement 2016), and many recently resettled households continue to await cash grants and housing materials to rebuild their homes. An impact investment of a housing program demonstrated that recipients were likely to go into debt because of the need to restore basic household consumption items (Gunasekara et al. 2016).

Second, gaps remain in addressing the specific needs of women affected by the war. Women in conflict affected areas are more vulnerable and relatively disadvantaged. Several thousand war widows are still without access to resources, infrastructure and housing, basic facilities and vocational skills and livelihoods to support their families (Asian Development Bank, Deutsche Gesellschaft fuer Internationale Zusammenarbeit 2015). Women face difficulties with respect to land rights (Asian Development Bank, Deutsche Gesellschaft fuer Internationale Zusammenarbeit 2015). While during the war, women's economic roles expanded, the postwar realities have reinforced restrictive gender norms, with women facing increased exposure to gender-based violence. Women, as well as men, have faced war-related traumas that often remain unresolved and continue to impact social relationships, community cohesion, and employment (Somasundaram and Sivayokan 2013).

Third, the delivery of relief and recovery programs have been centrally designed, with generally minimal inputs and participation from local populations. While postconflict rehabilitation and reconstruction is often implemented through a state led approach, many of the programs focused on physical infrastructure and were not used to concurrently bolster the economic, social and political empowerment of people and local communities (Keerawella 2013). Field-level assessments indicated that many local people viewed themselves as excluded from the recovery and reconstruction process, and cited examples of programs that were not specifically tailored to local needs and priorities. This situation is exacerbated by Sri Lanka's current institutional setup, which possesses two service delivery arms: the central government linked to line ministries, and the local government. This system leads to a duplication of efforts on the ground and lacks downward accountability to local communities, further compounding alienation from reconstruction efforts.

Finally, gaps remain in the implementation of several key reconciliation programs. The National Policy and Comprehensive Framework of Action on Education and Social Cohesion and Peace was developed in 2008, but the process to revise the curriculum has been slow. The Lessons Learnt and

Reconciliation Commission (2011) proposed several institutional, administrative and legislative measures designed to promote national unity and reconciliation, but these measures have not yet been adopted. In 2012, the Ministry of National Languages and Social Integration produced a National Policy Framework for Social Integration, under the theme "Social Cohesion Through Access to Everyone," in six areas—education, economic activities and employment, justice and legal resources, safe and secure social environment, safe and secure physical environment, and political participation (Asian Development Bank, Deutsche Gesellschaft fuer Internationale Zusammenarbeit 2015)—but progress on the implementation of these efforts is slow.

CONCLUSION

Since 2009, significant investments have been made in recovery and relief efforts in the postwar areas of the Northern and Eastern provinces, with a view to restore infrastructure and livelihoods among the affected populations. These efforts have primarily targeted physical infrastructure, including roads, bridges, schools, hospitals, and housing, thus changing the landscape of the Northern and Eastern provinces today (Keerawella 2013). However, other dimensions of the postwar recovery continue to be important, including social and economic well-being and governance and participation. Broader efforts at reconciliation are laudable, but implementation is lagging. While some gaps remain, the relative peace and stability of the region call for a transition towards efforts that promote local economic development, with a priority focus on growth and employment.

NOTES

1. This figure includes financing of government programs, as well as programs funding non-governmental organizations or other nonstate actors (e.g., mine clearing programs financed by outside sources).
2. These numbers were provided by the Ministry of Resettlement, Sri Lanka. See http://www .resettlementmin.gov.lk.
3. Includes government expenditures and development partner and donor assistance.

REFERENCES

Annual Update on Resettlement 2016. Ministry of Resettlement, Government of Sri Lanka.

Asian Development Bank, Deutsche Gesellschaft fuer Internationale Zusammenarbeit. 2015. "Country Gender Assessment Sri Lanka: An Update." ADB and GIZ. https://openaccess .adb.org.

de Mel, N., and R. Venugopal. 2016. *Peacebuilding Context Assessment: Sri Lanka 2016*. United Nations Sri Lanka, Colombo.

Gunasekara, V., M. Philips, K. Romeshun, and M. Munas. 2016. "'Life and Debt': Assessing the Impacts of Participatory Housing Reconstruction in Post-Conflict Sri Lanka." *Stability: International Journal of Security and Development* 5 (1): 10.

Kay, Alexander. 2015. "Post Conflict Measures and the Cost of Rebuilding Sri Lanka," 6th paper submitted by the International Criminal Law Bureau to the Office of the High Commissioner for Human Rights (OHCHR) concerning its investigation on Sri Lanka (OISL).

http://www.internationallawbureau.com/wp-content/uploads/2015/08/Post-Conflict-Costs-Sri-Lanka-Draft-6-.pdf.

Keerawella, G. 2013. *Post-War Sri Lanka: Is Peace a Hostage of the Military Victory?: Dilemmas of Reconciliation, Ethnic Cohesion, and Peace-Building.* Research Paper 8. Colombo: International Centre for Ethnic Studies.

Lessons Learnt and Reconciliation Commission. 2011. "Report of the Commission of Inquiry on Lessons Learnt and Reconciliation" November 2011. http://slembassyusa.org/downloads/LLRC-REPORT.pdf.

Somasundaram, D. and S. Sivayokan. 2013. "Rebuilding Community Resilience in a Post-War Context: Developing Insight and Recommendations—A Qualitative Study in Northern Sri Lanka." *International Journal of Mental Health Systems* 73.

4 Current Economic Dynamics in Postwar Sri Lanka

Nearly a decade after the end of Sri Lanka's civil war, the Northern and Eastern provinces have made strides in economic growth and development, thanks to significant investments in critical infrastructure. This section outlines the current economic dynamics of the two provinces. It finds that gross domestic product (GDP) growth rates have been strong, and both provinces have seen decreases in aggregate income inequality, as well as improvements in several multidimensional indicators of poverty.[1] Despite this progress, provincial contributions to GDP remain low, the competitiveness of the agriculture sector continues to be weak, and private-sector growth is lagging. Geographic pockets of poverty persist, and unemployment remains a challenge. As the Northern and Eastern provinces transition from recovery to local economic development, there is a need to look at their current comparative advantages in order to spur growth and development.

CURRENT ECONOMIC PROFILES OF THE NORTHERN AND EASTERN PROVINCES

With the end of the armed conflict, economic growth has been strong in the Northern and Eastern provinces. For example, between 2009 and 2010, growth in the Northern Province was 22.9 percent, and the Eastern Province was 15.9 percent, as compared to a national GDP growth rate of 3.5 percent for the same year. Agricultural production rose by 7 percent and fish production grew by 57 percent in the same period (Central Bank of Sri Lanka 2016). This upward trend has continued, with the Northern Province exhibiting positive economic growth rates through the latest available data. With the removal of the economic embargo, there is now a free flow of goods, services and people between the Northern and Eastern provinces and the rest of the country. This has resulted in price convergence, an influx of goods and services, and stimulated economic growth (World Bank 2009).

However, the GDP contribution of the two provinces to the national economy remains low, even when compared with the prewar situation. Much of

FIGURE 4.1

Share of provincial GDP to national GDP, 2014

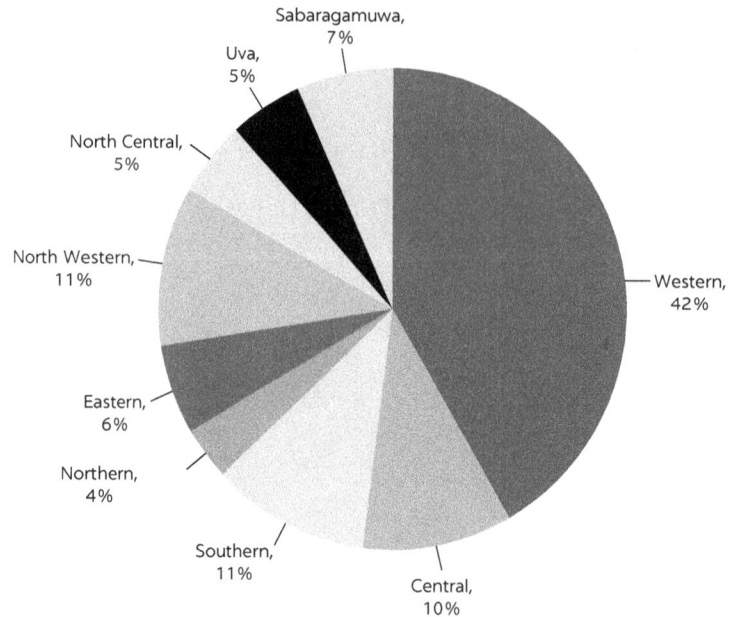

Source: Central Bank of Sri Lanka 2016.
Note: GDP = gross domestic product.

Sri Lanka's economic growth and production continues to center around the Western Province[2] (Central Bank of Sri Lanka 2016); the Western Province holds 25 percent of the population, and has more than 50 percent of the country's physical infrastructure concentrated in five percent of the country's land area. The Western and the adjoining Central, Southern and North Western provinces account for 70 percent of national GDP contributions. Respectively, the Northern and Eastern provinces contribute to only 3.6 and 5.7 percent of Sri Lanka's GDP, some of the lowest contributions in the country (figure 4.1).

The Provincial Gross Domestic Products (PGDPs)[3] also show differences between the Northern and Eastern provinces and the rest of the country. The end of the war saw PGDPs in the Northern and Eastern provinces that were, by monetary levels, some of the lowest in the country.[4] Since 2009, both the Northern and Eastern provinces have shown strong economic growth: the Northern Province's PGDP grew by 58 percent over five years (2009–14) and the Eastern Province's PGDP grew by 55 percent in the same period. This was slightly higher than Sri Lanka's national rate of growth over the same period (53.7 percent), indicating that much of the growth was distributed more evenly throughout the country (Central Bank of Sri Lanka 2016).

The economic structure of the Northern and Eastern provinces mirrors that of Sri Lanka, with the largest contribution to GDP coming from services (61 percent in the Northern Province and 50 percent in the Eastern Province). Industry is more prevalent in the Eastern Province, contributing to around 31 percent of GDP, whereas the equivalent figure is 19 percent in the Northern Province. Both economies show larger contributions to GDP from the agriculture sector (13 percent and 12 percent in the Northern and Eastern provinces, respectively), versus only 8 percent for the country as a whole (figure 4.2).

FIGURE 4.2

GDP by economic sector in the Northern and Eastern provinces, 2014

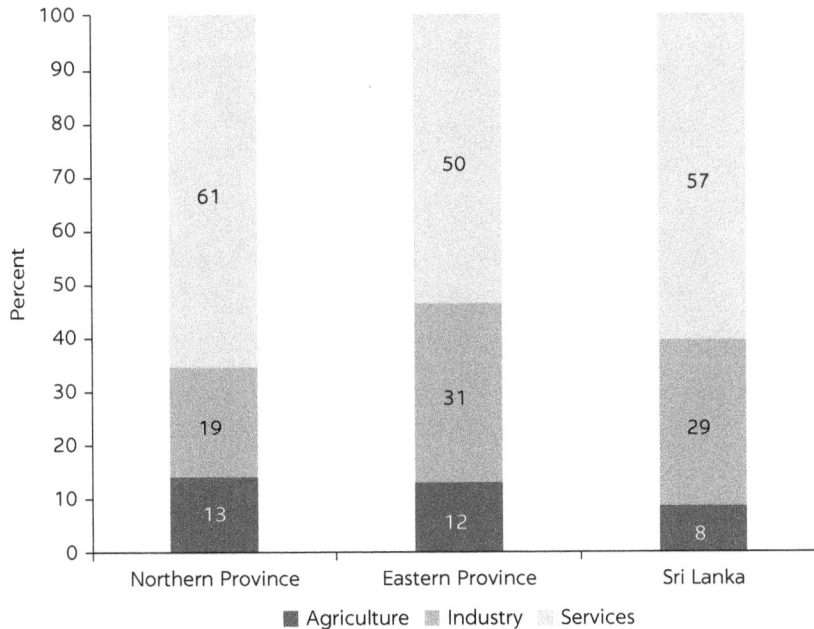

Source: Central Bank of Sri Lanka 2016.
Note: GDP = gross domestic product.

Since 2009, the trend away from the agriculture sector has remained consistent for both the Northern and the Eastern provinces. In the Northern Province, the sectoral contribution of agriculture to PGDP declined from 18.3 to 13 percent between 2009 and 2014. At the same time, there was a shift toward the industrial sector, with a rise in industry from 9.3 percent to 19.0 percent. The services sector declined slightly, from 72.3 to 61.3 percent. In the Eastern Province, the economy shifted further toward the services sector, with the share of this sector increasing from 43.6 to 49.7 percent. Industry declined only slightly, from 33.5 to 31.0 percent, and contributions from the agriculture sector nearly halved, from 22.9 to 12.5 percent (Central Bank of Sri Lanka 2016).

Within the services sector in both the Northern and Eastern provinces, there is growth in the transportation and communications, and wholesale and retail trade subsectors, reflecting a growing private-sector industry. However, contributions from the public administration and defense subsector continue to account for 20.5 percent of the Northern Province's services sector, which is more than twice the national figure (9.3 percent). The Northern and Eastern provinces are the only two provinces where public administration and defense are one of the top three categories contributing to the services sector (Central Bank of Sri Lanka 2016).

Comparative prosperity and poverty

Investments in regional development programs focused on post war recovery have had positive impacts on infrastructure at the provincial level. The Central Bank's subindicator on socioeconomic infrastructure shows convergence between the Northern and the Eastern provinces and the rest of the country between 2009 and 2014 (maps 4.1 and 4.2).

MAP 4.1

Socioeconomic infrastructure subindex by province, 2009

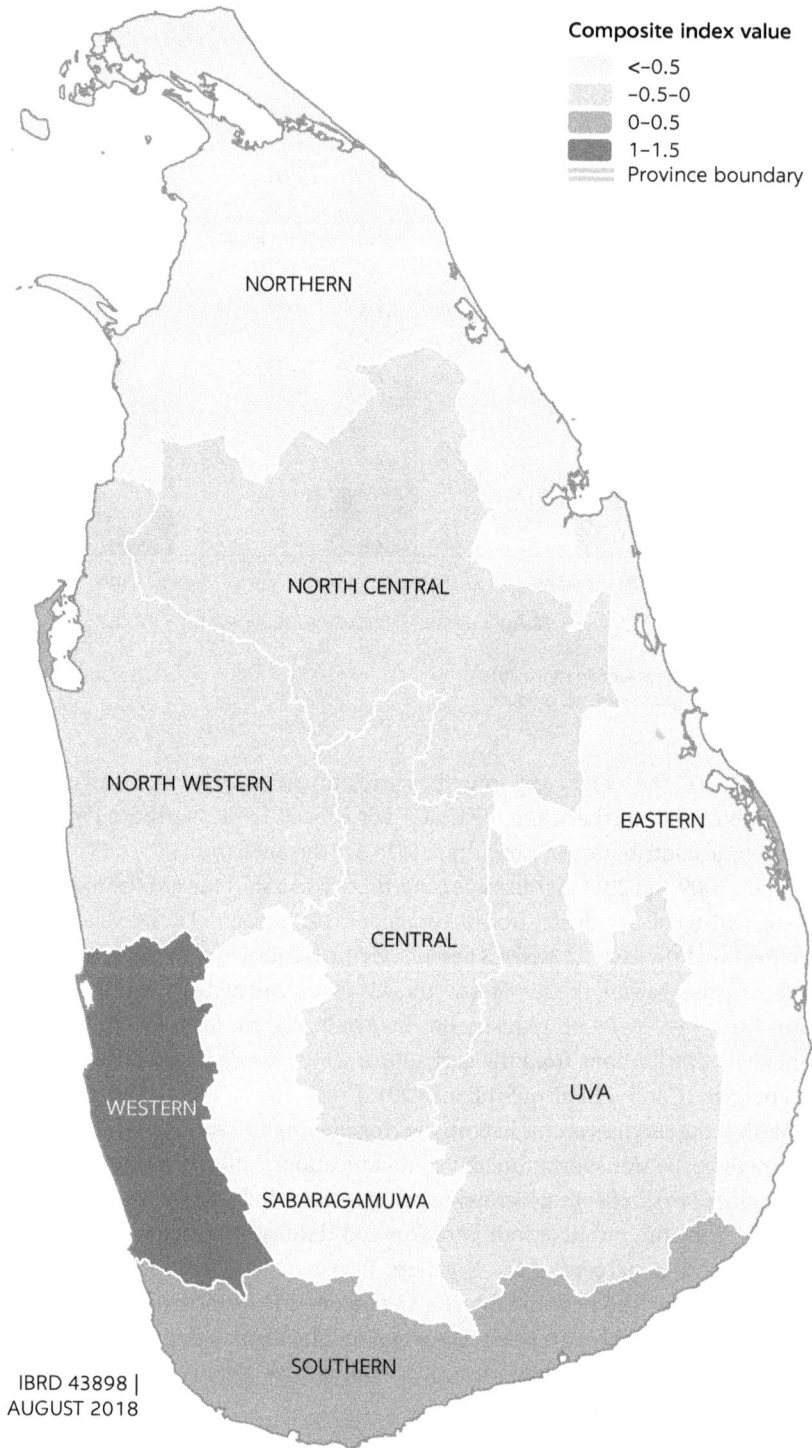

Source: Central Bank of Sri Lanka 2017.

Note: Sri Lanka's prosperity index is a composite indicator developed and maintained by the Central Bank of Sri Lanka, that measures and compares the level of prosperity of the country and across its provinces. It is made up of three subindices, including the Economy and Business Climate, Well-being of the People, and Socioeconomic Infrastructure sub-indices. The Socioeconomic Infrastructure subindex includes data on pipe-borne water quality, female participation in civic activities, road coverage, availability of electricity, crime-free environment, and availability of Information and Communication Technology (ICT) facilities in schools. For more information, see Central Bank of Sri Lanka 2017.

MAP 4.2

Socioeconomic infrastructure subindex by province, 2014

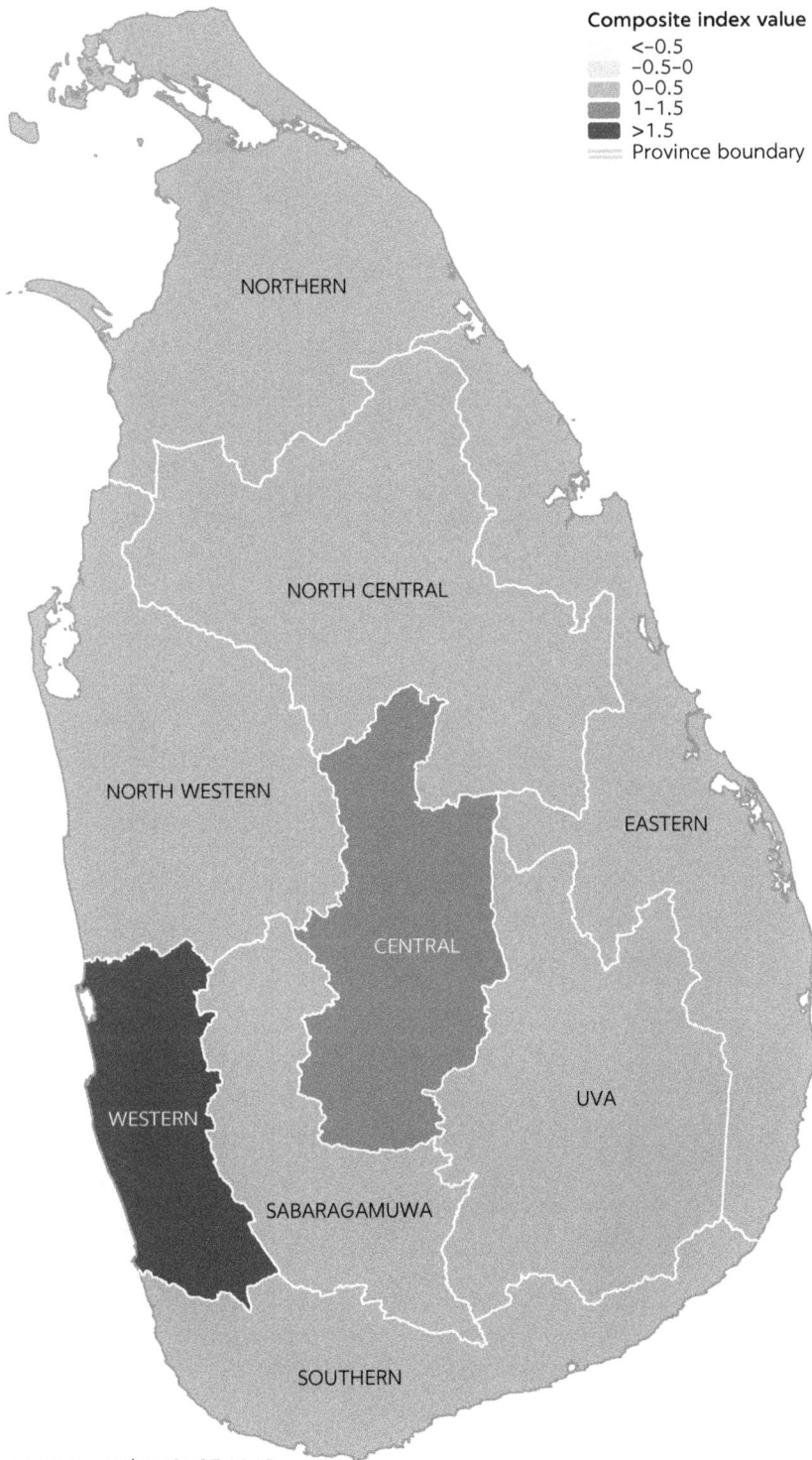

Composite index value
- <-0.5
- -0.5-0
- 0-0.5
- 1-1.5
- >1.5
- Province boundary

NORTHERN

NORTH CENTRAL

NORTH WESTERN

EASTERN

CENTRAL

UVA

WESTERN

SABARAGAMUWA

SOUTHERN

IBRD 43899 | AUGUST 2018

Source: Central Bank of Sri Lanka 2017.

Despite this, income disparities persist between the provinces, as shown in the maps below (maps 4.3 and 4.4), indicating that investments in physical infrastructure have not translated into reduced poverty among the populations of the Northern and Eastern provinces. In addition, within the Northern and Eastern

MAP 4.3

Income per capita by province, 2012/13

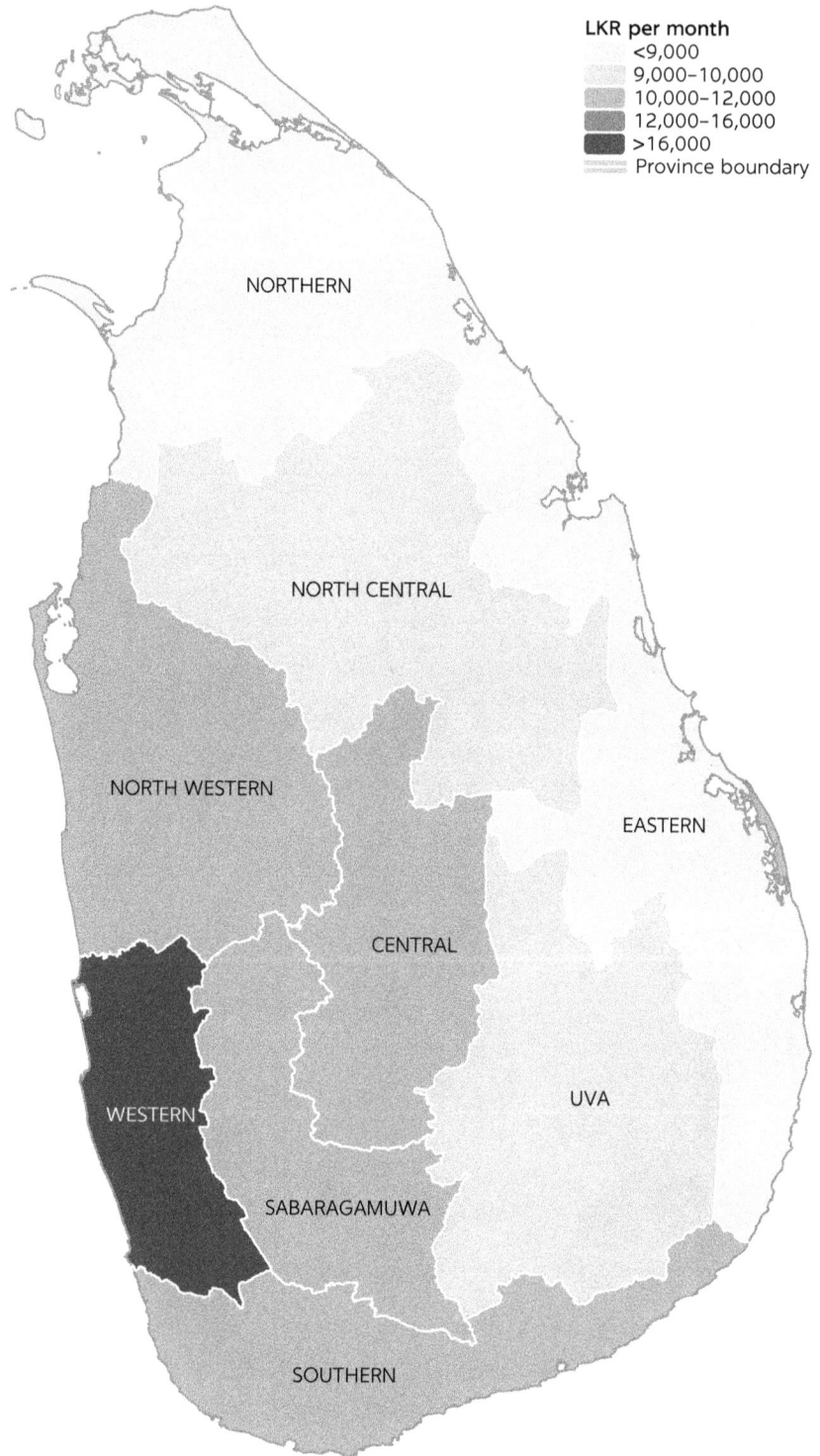

LKR per month
<9,000
9,000–10,000
10,000–12,000
12,000–16,000
>16,000
Province boundary

NORTHERN

NORTH CENTRAL

NORTH WESTERN

EASTERN

CENTRAL

WESTERN

UVA

SABARAGAMUWA

SOUTHERN

IBRD 43900 | AUGUST 2018

Source: Department of Census and Statistics 2013a.
Note: LKR = Sri Lankan Rupees

MAP 4.4

Poverty headcount index by division, 2012/13 HIES

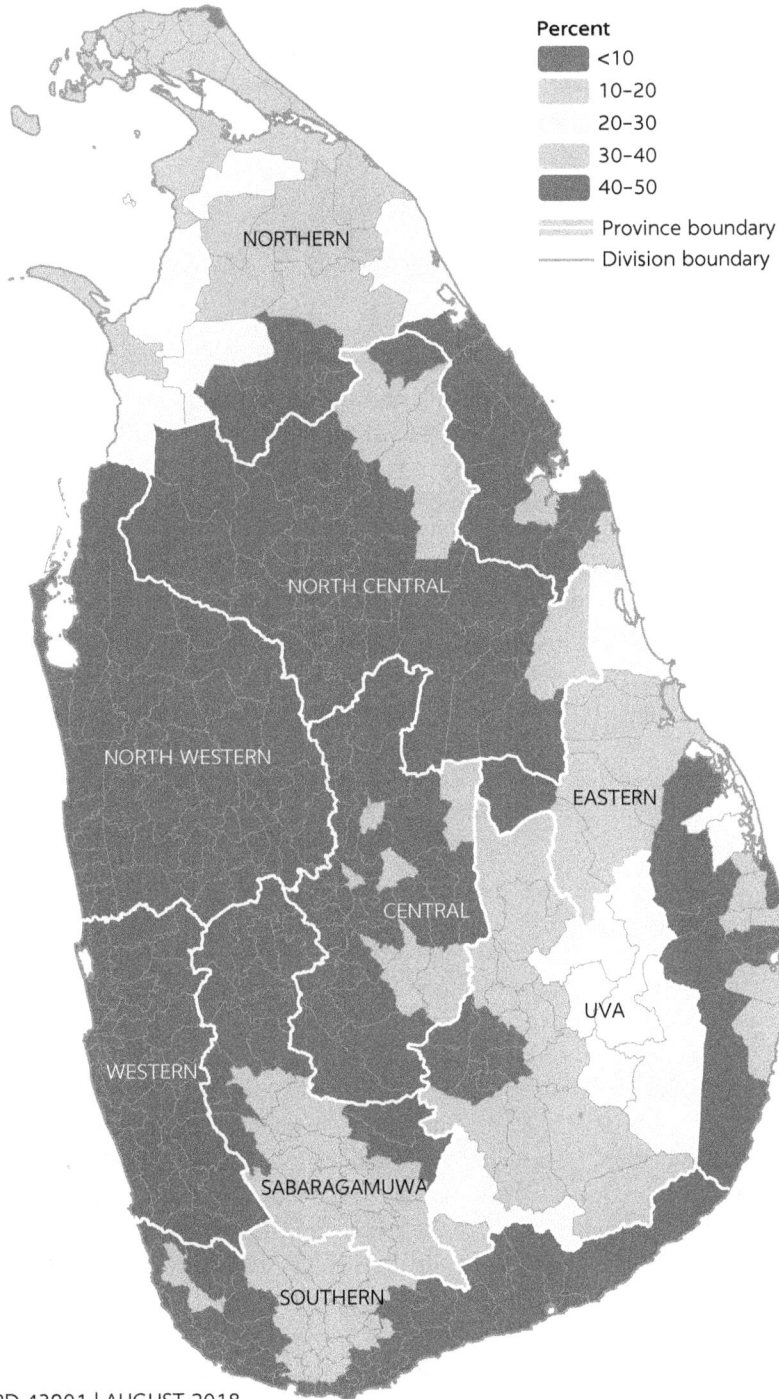

IBRD 43901 | AUGUST 2018

Source: Department of Census and Statistics 2013a.
Note: HIES = Household Income Expenditure Survey.

provinces, there are several emerging pockets of poverty. These indicate that there are entire geographic areas where economic growth and rejuvenation has simply not taken hold.

Overall, the above figures suggest that while significant investments have translated into improved infrastructure outcomes for the Northern and Eastern provinces, this has not led to improved incomes or local economic development for the area.

CURRENT ECONOMIC DYNAMICS

Current economic dynamics in the Northern and Eastern provinces continue to be linked both to the war and postwar recovery efforts to date. Specifically, the impact of the war and the economic embargo served to erode the competitiveness of the agriculture sector, and led to further declines in industry and private-sector investments that continue to be visible today. The collapse of the agriculture sector, coupled with the demographic impacts of the war, led to a shift toward daily wage labor and other informal sectors of the economy. Postwar recovery efforts have focused on small-scale activities aimed at stabilizing livelihoods and creating immediate job opportunities. As the Northern and Eastern provinces transition from postwar recovery interventions to medium term growth and development, there will be a need to restore the competitiveness of the vast agriculture sector, and to identify new sectors where the Northern and Eastern provinces demonstrate comparative advantages. New sectors for growth are particularly important to address growing unemployment among women and youth in the provinces

Agriculture

The agriculture sector remains the dominant productive sector in both the Northern and the Eastern provinces but competitiveness in the sector has been eroded (Northern Provincial Council 2016; Eastern Provincial Council 2016). In the Northern Province, paddy harvesting has been restored, with 31,483 hectares under cultivation and an estimated 75,000 hectares restored under irrigation facilities. The Eastern Province contributes 25 percent of national paddy production, 17 percent of national milk production and 21 percent of national fish production. However, destruction of irrigation infrastructure in the Eastern Province has slowed the overall growth rate of the agriculture sector, and contributions to the national economy remain low (Central Bank of Sri Lanka 2016).

While basic livelihoods and small-scale production of the agriculture sector have been largely restored, the effects of the war and the embargo served to erode the competitiveness of the agriculture sector. Sri Lanka's agriculture sector is changing, reflective of a growing urban population and changing food demands.[5] This has altered domestic agricultural supply chains (JICA 2013) and production, with greater competition and concentration of production geographically and among competitive producers. With the destruction of rural infrastructure, many of the farmers who have returned to agriculture in the Northern and Eastern provinces face greater competition from producers elsewhere in the country, as they must contend with broken irrigation infrastructure, poor rural roads and transportation networks, and limited storage facilities. Longstanding limits on fertilizers and other agricultural inputs changed production patterns among some farmers in the Northern and Eastern provinces, and limited support in agricultural extension services,[6] technical assistance and marketing support have also served to limit the potential growth of the sector. Similarly, potential growth of the fisheries sector was constrained by a general lack of access to credit, marketing and other facilities to support value addition at the local level. While early investments in livelihoods programs had looked to restore jobs in the short term, the lack of enabling infrastructure—such as marketing, business support, access to credit, etc.—is limiting the expansion of the sector. Today, around 30 percent of those employed in the Northern and Eastern provinces are in the agriculture sector, but many of them work at subsistence levels.

Field-level assessments also identified gender issues in the agriculture sector. With a relatively larger share of females during the war period, there was some evidence that gender norms were diluted, and women took on a greater role in agriculture and fishing. There is evidence to suggest that during the war, some livelihood programs did not account for this expanded role, and, instead, supported traditional genered roles in agriculture. In addition, many programs focused on the restoration of livelihoods in the agriculture sector were not able to address the broader issue of value chains that had been destroyed (Wanasundera 2006).

Agricultural land

Further compounding possible growth in the agriculture sector are the continued constraints on land. Lack of access to land is a key source of vulnerability. This is not just about the release of land from military occupation, but rather it is imperative that such land be made available to people for living and livelihood activities, as a means for stimulating local economic growth. Presently, one of the major challenges in restoring land to the people of the North and East is the lack of data on the precise status of land. Current data on the ownership status of land in the North and East, that is, whether it is state owned or privately owned, is poor. This lack of data often complicates claims to land and has led to the proliferation of land disputes (de Mel and Venugopal 2016). Access to land was impacted by the war, when displacement and the destruction of assets undermined small-scale production and agricultural livelihoods. With the end of the war, many internally displaced persons (IDPs) are returning to find their land encroached upon. Some cases were reported where privately held land had been declared forest land (based on field reports commissioned for this report).

Issues around access to land are also exacerbating gender vulnerabilities. Tamil and Muslim communities follow different customary land practices. For Tamils, the customary law, Tesawalami, governs the inheritance of property along matrilineal lines, and grants women the right to own property. However, control of the property is in the hands of a guardian, and a woman cannot invest in the property, mortgage, lease, or sell it without the prior permission of her husband or male guardian. Gender inequities in customary land laws have increased vulnerabilities in the Northern and Eastern provinces where women have the sole or primary responsibility for income generation through the cultivation of land or work as agricultural labor (Wanasundera 2006). Women are made vulnerable by their lack of documentation, inability to prove ownership, inability to dispose of land in the absence of their husband's death certification, and the nonrecognition by officials of women's altered status (Wanasundera 2006).

Industry and private-sector development

In the Northern and Eastern provinces, the legacy of the armed conflict has limited private investments, which are slowly recovering. Especially in the Northern Province, private-sector investment is limited, and largely focuses on energy, the garment sector, and manufacturing and trading, with limited growth in consumer facing industries (Economist Intelligence Unit 2015). According to the "Annual Survey of Industries" (Department of Census Statistics 2016), the Northern Province was estimated to have a total of 652 business establishments (3.2 percent of all establishments in Sri Lanka), and the Eastern Province had 782 establishments (3.8 percent of all establishments in Sri Lanka). Both provinces had low employment levels within these industries[7] and low output; the lowest percentage of industrial output was reported in the Northern Province. In addition, the value addition from establishments in both the Northern and the Eastern provinces was the lowest in the country (Department of Census and Statistics 2016).

While private-sector and industry investments continue to lag, there is some evidence that these are continuing to grow. Some of the reasons provided by firms for low investment levels are inadequate physical infrastructure; insufficient information on investment opportunities; a shortage of skilled workers; problems in obtaining land; and excessive red tape in obtaining investment approvals (Economist Intelligence Unit 2015). Employers in the Northern and Eastern provinces reported difficulty finding applicants to fill higher skilled vacancies, an issue that was reported more frequently than in other provinces (figure 4.3). Field assessments with industry and private-sector leaders confirmed skills shortages when seeking employees in the Northern and Eastern provinces. Workers in the Northern and Eastern provinces also self-reported lower literacy and numeracy skills, indicating a potentially greater skills mismatch among labor and industry in these provinces. In transitioning from a postwar recovery phase to a medium-term development program, the bottlenecks for industry and private-sector growth will need to be addressed.

LABOR AND EMPLOYMENT

Among the greatest impediments to the growth and development of the Northern and Eastern provinces identified during this assessment were labor and employment. As both provinces transition from recovery toward a longer-term development agenda, there will be a need to create more and better jobs, with a view to include women and youth in the labor force. This will necessitate efforts to address the specific challenges that women and youth face in joining the labor market, and to identify potential growth in sectors of comparative advantage for local economic development.

Unemployment remains the major challenge in the Northern and Eastern provinces. Despite relatively higher rates of poverty, labor force participation rates are much lower in the Northern and Eastern provinces (46 percent and 44 percent, respectively), as compared with the national average of 53 percent. Both the Northern and Eastern provinces have seen a gradual upward trend in employment rates since 2011, suggesting a broad recovery of the labor markets in these provinces (Department of Census and Statistics 2015). However, this broad growth masks some geographic and gender disparities in job creation.

FIGURE 4.3

Firms state inadequately educated workforce as a major or severe constraint

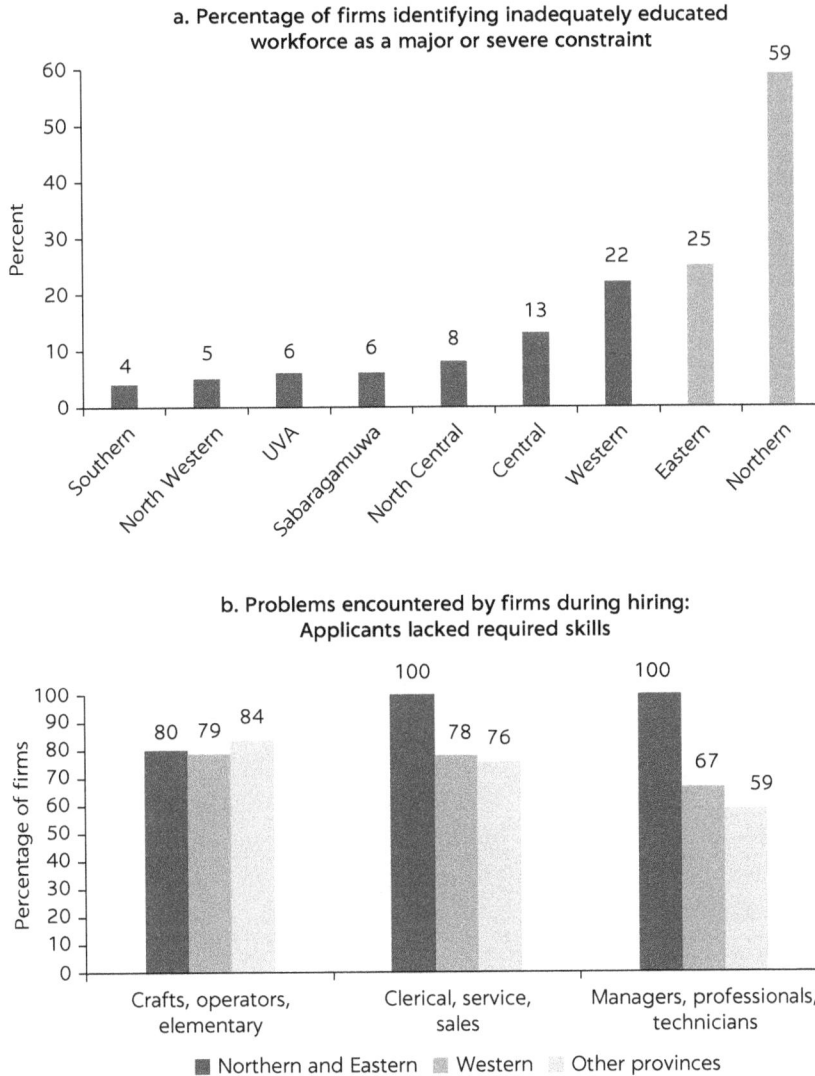

a. Percentage of firms identifying inadequately educated workforce as a major or severe constraint

b. Problems encountered by firms during hiring: Applicants lacked required skills

■ Northern and Eastern   ▨ Western   ▨ Other provinces

Source: Newhouse and Silwal 2017.

The Northern Province added around 78,000 jobs between 2011 and 2015, a 22 percent increase in the labor force, and the largest percentage increase in the country (table 4.1).[8] However, the jobs added to the labor force were predominantly concentrated in the Jaffna District and Vavuniya, two districts with relatively low poverty rates (table 4.2).[9] In the Eastern Province, job growth was predominantly in the industry sector (39,275 out of a total of 41,916 jobs added between 2011 and 2015), and the province saw a net loss in agriculture sector jobs. Within the manufacturing sector, most of the new jobs were concentrated in manufacturing and construction. In the Eastern Province, growth in employment was primarily concentrated in Batticaloa, followed by Trincomalee. Ampara experienced a net job loss between 2011 and 2015 (table 4.2). Generally, while job growth has been strong in both provinces, there is an uneven distribution of jobs—both in terms of geographic location and sector of the economy—with fewer jobs available to the semiskilled and unskilled labor force.

TABLE 4.1 **Job creation in Sri Lanka, by province, 2011–15**

PROVINCE	CHANGE IN NUMBER OF EMPLOYED PERSONS, 2011–15	PERCENTAGE CHANGE IN EMPLOYED PERSONS, 2011–15
Western	98,726	4.4
Central	105,281	10.8
Southern	25,927	2.7
Northern	78,513	22.1
Eastern	41,918	9.0
North Western	31,567	3.2
North Central	21,776	4.1
UVA	−70,602	−13.1
Sabaragamuva	9,168	1.1
Sri Lanka	342,272	4.4

Sources: Department of Census and Statistics 2011, 2015.
Note: The Labour Force Survey is conducted annually by the Department of Census and Statistics, government of Sri Lanka.

TABLE 4.2 **Job creation in the Northern and Eastern provinces, by district, 2011–15**

EMPLOYED POPULATION		
DISTRICT	NET CHANGE IN EMPLOYED PERSONS, 2011–15	PERCENTAGE CHANGE IN EMPLOYED PERSONS, 2011–15
Northern Province		
Jaffna	34,595	18.0
Kilinochchi	6,538	19.6
Mannar	16,140	24.9
Vavuniya	14,509	44.8
Mullaitivu	6,731	20.4
Eastern Province		
Batticaloa	25,979	16.9
Ampara	−3,307	−1.7
Trincomalee	19,245	16.0
Sri Lanka	**342,272**	**4.4**

Sources: Department of Census and Statistics 2011, 2015.
Note: The Labour Force Survey is conducted annually by the Department of Census and Statistics, government of Sri Lanka.

Despite strong job growth, labor force participation rates grew nominally, adversely affected by consistently low female labor force participation (FLFP). The FLFP rate is only 22 percent and 19 percent for the Northern and Eastern provinces, respectively, as compared to 35 percent at the national level (map 4.5). The districts with the lowest level of FLFP in the country were Kilinochchi, Vavuniya and Ampara. What is also of interest in the Northern and Eastern provinces is that low FLFP continues to be present in high poverty areas. Typically, higher poverty areas exhibit greater levels of FLFP, as more women will work to contribute to family income (map 4.6). However, in the Northern and Eastern provinces, even those districts with high levels of poverty display low rates of FLFP, including Jaffna, Kilinochchi, Mannar, Mullaitivu, Trincomalee,

MAP 4.5

Employment rates by gender and province, 2014

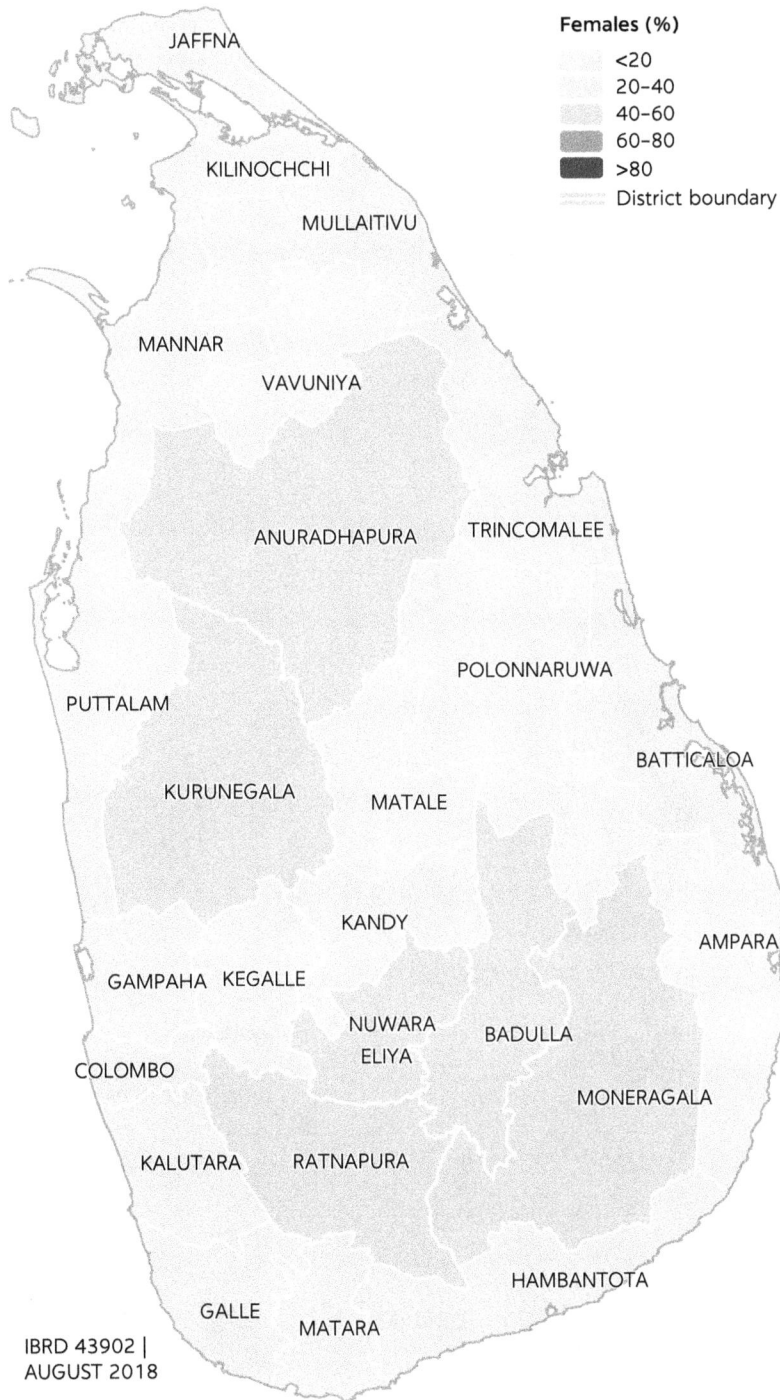

Females (%)

- <20
- 20–40
- 40–60
- 60–80
- \>80
- District boundary

JAFFNA

KILINOCHCHI

MULLAITIVU

MANNAR

VAVUNIYA

ANURADHAPURA

TRINCOMALEE

POLONNARUWA

PUTTALAM

BATTICALOA

KURUNEGALA

MATALE

KANDY

AMPARA

GAMPAHA KEGALLE

NUWARA
ELIYA

BADULLA

COLOMBO

MONERAGALA

KALUTARA

RATNAPURA

HAMBANTOTA

GALLE

MATARA

IBRD 43902 |
AUGUST 2018

Source: Solotaroff, Joseph, and Kuriakose 2018.

and Batticaloa. In fact, as maps 4.5 and 4.6 show, this pattern is unusual and unique to the Northern and Eastern provinces (maps 4.5 and 4.6).

This gender gap in labor force participation is also most pronounced among less educated women, and for middle aged women. Across districts in the Northern and Eastern provinces, there is low FLFP despite high poverty rates

MAP 4.6

Poverty headcount ratio and FLFP by district, 2013

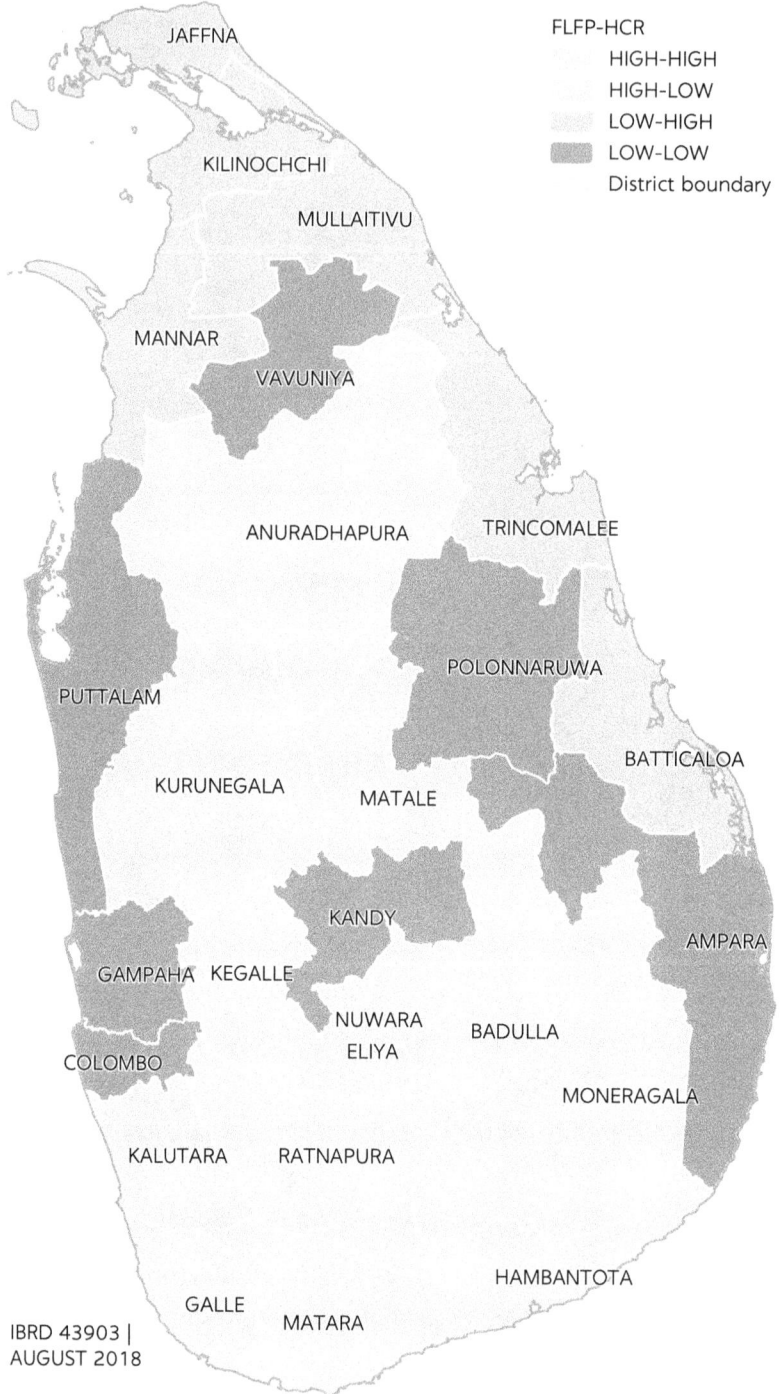

Source: Solotaroff, Joseph, and Kuriakose 2018.
Notes: FLFP = female labor force participation; HCR = headcount ratio.

(a pattern that does not hold true for other areas of high poverty). This is most pronounced in Batticaloa, Mullativu, Mannar, Jaffna, and Kilinochchi (Solotaroff, Joseph, and Kuriakose 2018). While poverty is not driving higher levels of FLFP across these districts, the inverse may be true—low FLFP in these areas may be contributing to higher poverty rates.

For women, there were several factors limiting their participation in the labor force. First is the availability of jobs that are commensurate with cultural norms for women. For example, fewer women were found in the agriculture sector in the Northern and Eastern provinces, and this was largely due to the gender gap in the fisheries sector; the gender gap in agricultural employment because of the fisheries sector was 41 percent in the Northern Province, and 23 percent in the Eastern Province, whereas it was only 16 percent for the country as a whole. Fisheries is typically a male dominated industry, with the role of women in the sector confined to specific tasks (Sireeranhan 2013).

Second, the lack of adequate transport and connectivity are significant barriers to FLFP in the Northern and Eastern provinces. Rural roads and transportation services are only slowly being restored, and many women cannot take up employment opportunities because of the distances they must travel. Women cited the need for jobs that were within a reasonable distance of their homes, in order to facilitate the double burden of working and domestic duties (Silva et al. 2018). The condition of secondary road networks and transportation networks are critical to facilitating women's participation in the labor force.

Finally, cultural norms, childcare and domestic duties often keep women away from formal employment opportunities. While this is not different from other parts of Sri Lanka, the specific cultural norms for Tamil and Muslim women—the predominant ethnic groups in the Northern and Eastern provinces—are arguably more conservative towards women working, particularly if it takes away from domestic duties and childcare (Solotaroff, Joseph, and Kuriakose 2018). On the other hand, the war did much to disrupt these cultural norms, and there is an opportunity now to support and facilitate women's entry into the labor market.

YOUTH

Youth employment is an issue throughout the country, and also in the Northern and Eastern provinces. While there has been some convergence between the Northern Province and the national average, youth employment in the Eastern Province has stayed relatively consistent and below national averages (figure 4.4). What is perhaps more worrisome is the general downward trend in youth employment that was seen between 2011 and 2015, and the fact that fewer youth are entering the labor market in general.

While youth throughout Sri Lanka face many challenges in the labor market, there are a number of issues that are specific to the Northern and Eastern provinces. First, the largest contributor to the youth-adult gap in employment rates in both provinces is returns to education, indicating that the lower education levels of youth in the Northern and Eastern provinces partly explain lower employment rates. A United Nations (UN) assessment also found that disruptions to schooling and training because of the war have resulted in a large number of young people who are less qualified and less equipped to take up the better paying jobs that are being created through new investments in war affected areas (de Mel and Venugopal 2016). The psychosocial assessment also found that children and youth face a higher incidence of psychological distress that negatively impacts their cognitive, emotional and intellectual development (Thowfeek 2017).

FIGURE 4.4

Youth participation in the labor force, 2011–15

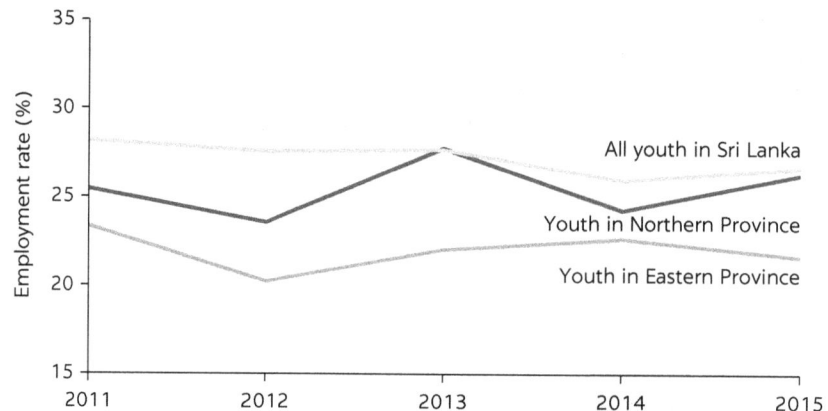

Source: Department of Census and Statistics 2011–15.
Notes: The Labour Force Survey is conducted annually by the Department of Census and Statistics, government of Sri Lanka. (Sample: 15–24 year olds)

The biggest issue cited for youth is the mismatch between aspirations and the availability of jobs. There is a reluctance to take up manual work or pursue training opportunities at the vocational level, and salary expectations remain relatively high (de Mel and Venugopal 2016). Youth, particularly educated youth, hold on to aspirations of a "good job," even when they are not available, and they are more likely to be unemployed (de Mel and Venugopal 2016). Especially in affluent parts of the Northern Province, there is a perception that unemployment is further supported through a remittance culture.[10] Similar to the patterns of FLFP, youth unemployment remains high, despite relatively high levels of poverty, which is dissimilar to other areas of Sri Lanka.[11]

According to the assessment conducted by del Mel and Venugoapal in 2016, the concept of a "good job" seems to have three elements: remuneration; job security; and designation (social status). This makes the pensionable and permanent jobs of the public sector highly attractive, especially as the starting wages in the public sector are also relatively high in relation to the private sector. This explains the disproportionate demand for public sector jobs over the private sector, and especially over manual work. Between 40 percent and 50 percent of those seeking jobs in the Northern and Eastern provinces are attempting to secure employment in the public sector, whereas the highest availability of new jobs seems to be in the manual work of the construction sector (de Mel and Venugopal 2016). It is also possible that jobs outside of the public sector, or opportunities for entrepreneurship and self-employment are not considered because of low awareness of these pathways, as well as the fact that social status is often shaped by parents and adults in the community.

In addition to the issue of high aspirations against a low availability of jobs, it was also noted that labor mobility in the Northern and Eastern provinces is low.[12] Part of this low labor mobility can be attributed to a lack of awareness and low information flows across localities. Part of the lower labor mobility outside of the Northern and Eastern provinces can also be attributed to language barriers; since most Tamil youth attend Tamil medium schools, they face challenges in participating in Sri Lanka's labor market, both in availing of jobs outside of Tamil speaking areas, or working for companies and businesses with a national or international focus.

CONCLUSIONS

The economies of the Northern and Eastern provinces have demonstrated strong growth since the end of the war in 2009. However, both provinces continue to demonstrate low levels of contribution to national GDP. The agriculture sector shows signs of low competitiveness, and private-sector investment and industrial growth are weak. Most notably, despite relatively high poverty rates, low labor force participation persists, especially for women and youth. The drive for improved employment opportunities in the Northern and Eastern provinces will necessitate going beyond investments to restore livelihoods. This will require maximizing employment creation through a more comprehensive set of supports (i.e., skills development, access to business development and microfinance services, market linkages) that bring sustainable employment. This should be particularly focused on the barriers to both female and youth employment. Complementary efforts focused on building the skill base of the local population, combined with regulatory and tax incentives, as well as a focus on local endowments or strategic emerging industries, could help to spur employment and further reduce poverty within the Northern and Eastern provinces.

NOTES

1. Improvements in Sri Lanka's Prosperity Index can be taken as indications of improvements in well being over time, as many indicators provide proxies for well being.
2. The Western Province alone holds 25 percent of the population, and has more than 50 percent of the country's physical infrastructure concentrated in five percent of the country's area. The Western and adjoining Central, Southern, and North Western provinces account for 70 percent of national (gross domestic products (GDP) contributions.
3. The PGDP for 2015 has been computed by the statistics department of the Central Bank of Sri Lanka (CBSL), based on the disaggregation of the rebased series of National Accounts estimates (2010 constant prices) by the Department of Census and Statistics (DCS), government of Sri Lanka.
4. In 2009, the PGDP of the Northern Province was SL Rs 156 billion, and the PGDP of the Eastern Province was SL Rs 279 billion.
5. JICA 2013. This study found that with growing competition between domestic and imported products, local agricultural supply chains have evolved towards two models: supermarket chains that directly purchase agricultural products from farmers, and agri-business companies that manage a series of stages from production and processing to retailing and exporting, with local producers capturing between 31 and 73 percent of the final prices.
6. Some reports emerged that in the vacuum of agricultural extension services, private chemical and fertilizer companies were providing advisory services on their products.
7. 11,571 in Northern Province and 13,201 in Eastern Province.
8. The Eastern Province added 41,918 jobs over the same period, or a 9 percent increase. This was against a total increase in Sri Lanka of 342,272 jobs, or a 4.4 percent increase in the labor force over the same period.
9. Based on calculations from the Sri Lanka Labour Force surveys 2011 and 2015. These surveys are conducted annually by the Department of Census and Statistics, government of Sri Lanka.
10. While a higher level of remittances was not found in the official statistics, it was reported that many of these remittances were sent using informal networks, so the precise amounts of remittances are unknown.
11. The other two provinces in Sri Lanka that have very high level of poverty—Uva and Sabaragamuwa—have among the highest levels of labor force participation rates: 61 and 55 percent, respectively (de Mel and Venugoapal 2016).
12. The UN Assessment identifies, for example, that the daily wage rate for unskilled workers exceeds LKR 1,000 in Jaffna, whereas, it tends to be around LKR 800, even in Colombo (see de Mel and Venugoapal 2016).

REFERENCES

Central Bank of Sri Lanka. 2017. "Sri Lanka Prosperity Index 2016." Government of Sri Lanka. https://www.cbsl.gov.lk/en/node/2490.

———. 2016. *Economic and Social Statistics of Sri Lanka*. Government of Sri Lanka.

de Mel, N., and R. Venugopal. 2016. *Peacebuilding Context Assessment: Sri Lanka 2016*. United Nations Sri Lanka, Colombo.

Department of Census and Statistics. 2011. *Sri Lanka Labour Force Survey*. Government of Sri Lanka.

———. 2012. *Sri Lanka Labour Force Survey*. Government of Sri Lanka.

———. 2013a. *Household Income and Expenditure Survey 2012/13*. Government of Sri Lanka.

———. 2013b. *Sri Lanka Labour Force Survey*. Government of Sri Lanka.

———. 2014. *Sri Lanka Labour Force Survey*. Government of Sri Lanka.

———. 2015. *Sri Lanka Labour Force Survey*. Government of Sri Lanka.

———. 2016. *Annual Survey of Industries*. Government of Sri Lanka.

Eastern Provincial Council. 2016. Statistical Information 2016. Eastern Provincial Council. Government of Sri Lanka. www.ep.gov.lk.

Economist Intelligence Unit. 2015. "Sri Lanka: Risk Assessment." http://country.eiu.com /article.aspx?articleid=1513530935&Country=Sri%20Lanka&topic=Risk&subtopic=_3.

JICA (Japan International Cooperation Agency). 2013. "Democratic Socialist Republic of Sri Lanka: Data Collection Survey on Agricultural Distribution Network and Marketing." http://open_jicareport.jica.go.jp/pdf/12115689.pdf.

Newhouse, David Locke, and Ani Rudra Silwal. 2018. "The State of Jobs in Post-conflict Areas of Sri Lanka (English)." Policy Research Working Paper 8355. World Bank, Washington, DC. http://documents.worldbank.org/curated/en/443541519651773814/The-state-of-jobs-in -post-conflict-areas-of-Sri-Lanka.

Northern Provincial Council. 2016. Statistical Information, Northern Provincial Council, Government of Sri Lanka. www.np.gov.lk.

Silva, T., D. Herath, R. Thowfeek, S. Sivakanthan, and V. Kunanayahan. 2018. Livelihood Trends *Background Paper No 1 to the World Bank Socio-Economic Assessment of the Northern and Eastern Provinces*, International Centre for Ethnic Studies, Colombo.

Sireeranhan, A. 2013. "Participation of Family-Women in Agricultural Production: A Case Study of Jaffna District, Sri Lanka." *Journal of Economics and Sustainable Development* 4 (13): 143–147.

Solotaroff, Jennifer L., George Joseph, and Anne Kuriakose. 2018. *Getting to Work: Unlocking Women's Potential in Sri Lanka's Labor Force*. Directions in Development—Countries and Regions. Washington, DC: World Bank.

Thowfeek, R. 2018. "Psychosocial Assessment of the War Affected Northern and Eastern Provinces of Sri Lanka: distress and Growth Post-War." Background Paper 4, World Bank Socio-Economic Assessment of the Northern and Eastern Provinces of Sri Lanka, International Centre for Ethnic Studies, Colombo.

Wanasundera, L. 2006. *Rural Women in Sri Lanka's Post-Conflict Rural Economy*. Bangkok, Thailand: Food and Agriculture Organization of the United Nations, RAP Publication 2006/13. http://www.fao.org/3/a-ag114e.pdf.

World Bank. 2009. "Reshaping Economic Geography: Sri Lanka." World Bank, Washington, DC.

———. 2012. Enterprise Survey for Sri Lanka. World Bank, Washington, DC. http://www .enterprisesurveys.org/data/exploreeconomies/2011/sri-lanka.

5 Contemporary Social Issues and Demographic Changes in the Northern and Eastern Provinces

Social issues in the Northern and Eastern provinces are closely linked to the legacy of the war. These include the impacts of displacement on community institutions and social support mechanisms that continue to be weakened. In addition, changes in the demographic structure of the Northern and Eastern provinces continue to be visible, and are increasing gender vulnerabilities, especially among Tamil communities. There are widespread symptoms of trauma among the affected populations, including posttraumatic stress disorder (PTSD), alcoholism, and suicide. Emerging challenges center around addressing the needs of affected populations and mitigating horizontal inequalities.[1] Restoring trust and promoting political, social, and economic participation will continue to be priorities for advancing the objective of sustainable peace.

BREAKDOWN OF COMMUNITY STRUCTURES

On the social side, the effects of eroded community structures through multiple displacements and conflict, coupled with psychosocial challenges, has translated into cycles of alcoholism, suicide, and gender-based violence, especially among the poorer segments of the population. Rising indebtedness, linked to restoring assets lost in the war, as well as to poor financial literacy, further exacerbate the cycle of poverty and social issues. These social issues are visible throughout the Northern and Eastern provinces where geographic pockets of extreme deprivation prevail (de Mel and Venugopal 2016).

Nearly a decade after the end of the civil war, community and social structures remain weak throughout much of the Northern and Eastern provinces. Displacement, often in multiple instances and over several generations, served to weaken communal and community structures in these provinces. Since the end of the civil war, a slow process of resettling internally displaced persons (IDPs) and returning displaced populations is taking place. However, social and family structures continue to be weak. This is visible in the continued low levels of trust between and within local communities, as well as weak family structures.

TABLE 5.1 **Size and sex composition of the population in the Northern Province, 1981–2011**

YEAR	MALE	FEMALE	TOTAL	SEX RATIO
1981	562,851	546,553	1,109,404	102.9
2012	520,760	550,555	1,061,315	94.6

Sources: Department of Census and Statistics 1981, 2011.

Community groups throughout the Northern and Eastern provinces demonstrated a leadership deficit. In addition, widespread mistrust within and between communities is evidence of low levels of social capital and weak social ties and networks (Aldrich 2012). Relations between different ethnic and religious groups were particularly fractured, with some signs of increasing divisions and isolation between Muslim, Tamil and Sinhala communities. In the Northern Province, where 93 percent of the population is of the same ethnic group (Sri Lankan Tamil), there were fewer ethnic divisions, although there was some evidence of the re-emergence of caste structures, particularly in Jaffna.

Further evidence of weak social ties and deteriorating social structures was evident in the prevalence of changes in traditional family structures and growing marital instability (Herath 2018). While no formal statistics exist, field assessments found evidence of the increased prevalence of extra-marital affairs, husbands with multiple families, abandonment,[2] and growing marital problems—including separations and divorce. These changes were attributed to two factors. First, multiple displacement, the disintegration of social networks, and the state of flux in settlements and IDP camps led to changes in strict social codes and norms around the institutions of family and marriage. Second, the skewed sex ratio and relative surplus of women that has emerged as a result of the war (table 5.1) has reduced women's bargaining power within and around the institution of marriage, leading to greater marital instability and the breakup of family institutions. This is in line with findings from studies on gender relationships and skewed sex ratios conducted elsewhere in the world (Herath 2018).

SKEWED SEX RATIOS AND GENDER VULNERABILITY

The skewed sex ratio and relative surplus of women is also contributing to greater vulnerability and insecurity for women throughout the Northern and Eastern provinces. In field assessments, women noted that it was difficult to raise a dowry, that there is a notable deficit of marriageable male partners of appropriate ages in the civilian population, and the weakening of the bargaining position of girls vis-à-vis young men in the local marriage market.[3] This is contributing to both consensual and nonconsensual sexual alliances involving women who have limited agency or ability to negotiate. Unmarried women are seen as a burden to the family, and unmarried women past the marriageable age experience a complex mix of stigma, vicious rumors and potential abuse.[4] Other vulnerable groups are women headed households and widows, who by local customs and traditions are prohibited from remarrying. With the breakdown of strict social norms and the relative surplus of men reducing women's bargaining power, households without a male resident are targeted by men for extra-marital relationships, harassment or abuse. Estimates of the percentage of households with serious marital problems, including separations and divorces, ranged from 10 to 25 in selected communities in the Northern and Eastern provinces.

DISPLACEMENT

Displacement and resettlement of the local population has been a feature of the past few years in the Northern and Eastern provinces. By government estimates, 4,779.8 hectares have been released from military control or as high security zones back to the local population, and 887,400 people have been resettled as of December 30, 2016.[5] Resettled households are offered packages of support that include housing, although many families are reporting that long wait times for the benefits, coupled with the limited provision of infrastructure, are making recovery slow. With the influx of microcredit in the postwar period, many households are taking loans in an effort to smooth consumption or to purchase household items (Gunasekara et al. 2016). The availability of credit was generally perceived as a positive development throughout the field-level research that was conducted for the purposes of this report. However, the lack of financial literacy among the local population, coupled with perceived aggressive lending techniques,[6] is resulting in the increased indebtedness of local households (table 5.2).[7]

TABLE 5.2 **Debt is a larger share of household consumption in the Northern and Eastern provinces and tends to be informal**

	NORTHERN PROVINCE	EASTERN PROVINCE	WESTERN PROVINCE	OTHER PROVINCES
Household had debt from the following source (%)				
Banks	28	24	26	31
Finance companies	5	8	10	8
Money lenders	10	16	8	6
Pawning of assets	36	41	44	39
Retail shops	17	24	9	17
Any kind of debt	**63**	**69**	**69**	**67**
Indebted households only:				
Share of total household debt from each source (%)				
Banks	30	23	24	30
Finance companies	4	5	9	8
Money lenders	8	11	5	4
Pawning of assets	43	44	43	39
Retail shops	8	10	4	9
Other (credit card, employer, installment)	7	7	15	10
All household debt	**100**	**100**	**100**	**100**
Debt as a share of annual household consumption (%)				
Banks	16	11	14	12
Finance companies	4	6	7	5
Money lenders	6	5	2	1
Pawning of assets	28	22	16	13
Retail shops	0	1	0	0
Other (credit card, employer, installment)	2	2	4	5
All household debt	**56**	**47**	**43**	**36**

Source: Newhouse and Silwal 2018.

Official figures on suicide and attempted suicide show a spike in 2014[8] in some districts in the Northern Province, which could be related, in part, to household indebtedness and economic factors. Field assessments indicated a perception that indebtedness was related to suicide, especially for women.

Displaced populations were more likely to show high rates of unresolved psychosocial needs, including higher rates of depression, anxiety, and PTSD. Field assessments indicated high levels of trauma symptoms among the local population. Recent studies measuring exposure to trauma found that those with greater exposure to traumatic events were more likely to exhibit symptoms of trauma, including depression, anxiety, and PTSD. These traumatic events include experiencing torture; injury from a landmine; separation from family; lack of food, water, or shelter; and loss or destruction of property and belongings, among others. The experience of trauma was the greatest explanatory factor for experiencing mental health symptoms (Jayasuriya et al. 2016).

POSTWAR TRAUMA

Nearly a decade after the war ended, many mental health and psychosocial issues continue to be visible among the populations in the Northern and Eastern provinces. A 2016 nationwide survey of mental distress in Sri Lanka compares populations in the country based on exposure to conflict and looks at metrics of mental health (n=18,182). The findings demonstrated that individuals living in moderate to severe conflict zones had experienced higher rates of food scarcity and job loss as compared to those living in minimal conflict zones—both possible risk factors for mental health and psychosocial issues. There was no difference in terms of access to health care or police services. As expected, a greater proportion of respondents exposed to the war spent more time in camps for internally displaced persons as compared to those in minimal conflict areas (Jayasuriya et al. 2016).

As the table below demonstrates, exposure to conflict increases the prevalence of mental health symptoms, including depression and anxiety (table 5.3). In the case of depression, individuals living in moderate to severe conflict zones were three to four times more likely to experience symptoms. With anxiety, the incidence doubled as the exposure to conflict became more severe. These findings demonstrate empirically that prolonged exposure to conflict continues to affect mental health in Sri Lanka today.

The authors also found that providing opportunities for employment "not only helps to overcome poverty and food insecurity but might also help restore meaningful roles and a sense of identify that help in the rebuilding of a social fabric" (Jayasuriya et al. 2016, 8). Access to mental health care is still relatively

TABLE 5.3 **Indicators of depression and anxiety by exposure to conflict in Sri Lanka, 2016**

Percent

INDICATOR/SEVERITY OF CONFLICT EXPOSURE	ALL PARTICIPANTS	MINIMAL	MODERATE	SEVERE
Depression	12	10	33	40
Anxiety	14	13	23	23

Source: Jaysuriya et al. 2016.

limited in the war-affected regions of Sri Lanka. Most schools do not have properly trained counseling staff for children, and according to a doctor in the Mannar district, "...Depression and PTSD are going on, especially in women-headed households, in all districts." It is widely believed that more investment in mental health is necessary. Interestingly, this study also measured coping mechanisms. For those who were displaced or resettled, it was believed that more income (25.5 percent of displaced and 37.8 percent of resettled respondents), as well as employment (30.9 percent of displaced and 23.2 percent of resettled respondents) would help to restore mental health. Field-level assessments commissioned as background for this study also confirmed a need for increased counseling to address trauma among the affected populations.

Suicide and alcoholism

Other symptoms of postwar trauma included high rates of suicide and alcoholism. Field-level assessments suggested that rates of suicide and alcoholism were high, particularly among the Tamil population. District level data from 2011 on suicide rates did confirm higher than average crude suicide rates in several districts in the Northern and Eastern provinces.[9] Many respondents identified depression related to economic factors as being instrumental in attempted suicides and deaths resulting from suicide. The inability to engage in meaningful livelihoods and economic activity, together with the repressive elements of the social environment—such as constant fear and anxiety, harassment and hopelessness—are identified as risk factors for attempted suicides and completed suicides.[10] Relative to districts in other provinces, alcohol consumption is consistently elevated in Northern and Eastern districts. Respondents reported the prevalence of high levels of alcoholism, especially in Tamil communities (around 90 percent of respondents in focus group discussions (FGDs) reported alcohol consumption by males), and that alcoholism increased substantially during and after the war. Apart from diverting income away from the household, it was also reported that alcoholism contributed to domestic violence, other forms of gender-based violence, health problems and family breakdown. Smaller-scale health studies relate the increased consumption of alcohol to postwar trauma[11] (Thowfeek 2018).

Gender-based violence

The prevalence of alcohol consumption and alcoholism was closely linked with gender-based violence throughout the Northern and Eastern provinces. Field-level research revealed a perception that gender-based violence is prevalent in all households, with estimates of violence occurring in around 90 percent of families. Since the majority of this violence goes unreported, it is difficult to corroborate those figures. Jaffna District conducted a specific study on gender-based violence and found that 300 cases were reported annually since 2011, mostly related to male violence against women (Jaffna District 2012). While domestic and gender-based violence often goes unreported, the assessment found several points related to the Northern and Eastern provinces that are worth noting. First, the lack of employment opportunities, along with the skewed sex ratio and relative surplus of females, is linked to the vulnerability of women within the household, including their weakened negotiating and bargaining power. It was noted that when women were unemployed, they faced a higher incidence of violence in the household as compared to employed women.[12] Second, while many divisions have set up gender-based-violence desks, many survivors of violence were unaware of the support services available to them, or they were hesitant to use such services because of mistrust. Many of the Tamil informants highlighted a language barrier with Sinhala officials, which further reduced the incidence of reporting (Herath 2018).

Intergenerational transmission

The deterioration of family structures, community institutions, and the resulting increases in suicide, alcoholism and abuse are of particular concern because of their effect on youth, as they perpetually struggle to redefine their place in family and society (Gunatilaka, Mayer, and Vodopivec 2010). Perceptions in the Northern and Eastern provinces of a growing "youth problem" could be linked to the intergenerational transmission of violence, particularly if rates of domestic violence are as high as those reported during focus group discussions. Global studies have shown that witnessing violence between parents as a child is a risk factor for women experiencing violence from their own partners as adults, and for men perpetrating violence against their partners (World Bank 2011). One small-scale study conducted in the Northern and Eastern provinces in 2008 (n=296) demonstrated the incidence of PTSD and major depression among children affected by the war and natural disaster. It also showed that children were more prone to PTSD and depression if their father had a higher degree of war exposure and increased levels of alcohol consumption (Catani et al. 2008). Overall, while there is no conclusive evidence that domestic violence or the deterioration of family and social structures is linked to higher rates of psychological problems in affected children specific to the Northern and Eastern provinces, there is enough global evidence of these trends to highlight the risks of continued psychosocial distress persisting among the next generation in the Northern and Eastern provinces.

VULNERABLE POPULATIONS

Several specific groups within the Northern and Eastern provinces continue to be vulnerable outside of socioeconomic and poverty metrics. These populations include the physically disabled, female headed households, widows, ex-combatants, orphans, children, and the elderly. While the actual numbers of any of these individual groups are perhaps not large, the specific challenges they face are legacies of Sri Lanka's civil war. In addition, many of these vulnerable populations were identified as being predominantly concentrated in the Tamil community, highlighting emerging horizontal inequalities. Details on several of these groups are provided below, followed by a discussion on horizontal inequalities.

The vulnerabilities of female headed households and widows have already been described in the previous section on gender vulnerabilities. However, it is also worth noting here that widows and female headed households face specific challenges with regard to cultural norms that prohibit remarriage. This affects household income and places households at risk of falling below the poverty line. Female headed households and widows with underage children in the household were also cited as being less food secure, and there were also, higher levels of childhood anemia, and child malnutrition. No recent data was available to substantiate any trends over time, but the widespread mention of child malnutrition as a growing issue is cause for concern, particularly when considering the potential long term cognitive and health effects of child malnutrition (Vincius et al. 2011).

The deterioration of family institutions also negatively affects underage children in the household. There was an increase in the reporting of orphaned children, children left with one or another parent, and children left with extended relatives or neighbors. This has put underage children at further risk of abuse within the household. A recent United Nations profile from the Eastern Province showed a rise in reported child abuse cases since 2011; between 2012 and 2014, the number of child abuse cases reported increased from 441 to 854. Of the child abuse cases, 32 percent involve sexual abuse. While some of the increases in reporting may be due to a greater availability of helpdesks, field-level research also confirmed perceptions that a growing number of children are facing issues of malnutrition, abuse, and abandonment. In addition, reports of child abuse, neglect, and exploitation are likely underreported, in part because of sociocultural factors (Sathiadas, Viswalingam, and Vijayaratnam 2018).

Disabled people were also identified as a vulnerable population, and several stakeholders indicated that the government has yet to fully address their needs. No updated figures on the number of disabled persons were available at the time of writing, but several studies point to adverse impacts on physical health from the war, including the incidence of physical trauma, such as spinal cord injuries, amputations and other disabilities (Somasundaram and Sivayokan 2013). It was reported that disabled people have trouble holding down jobs and accessing higher education, due in part to discrimination, which naturally leads to high levels of poverty.

Several stakeholders brought attention to the lack of high-quality care and attention for children, the elderly and the disabled. Field-level research generally revealed the belief that families neglect the elderly, and that not enough resources are devoted to their care. The breakdown of traditional family structures that had historically ensured care for the elderly contributes to their lack of care and support. It was also reported that the elderly, particularly elderly women, face difficulties in finding employment and accessing credit (based on field research conducted as background for this study, 2017).

Finally, ex-combatants were identified as one of the most vulnerable populations. While over 11,000 of around 12,000 ex-combatants have returned to their homes or communities, they continue to face social stigma and difficulties in finding employment. This is more pronounced for the approximately 2,240 female ex-combatants, who face additional stigma and gender discrimination. Social stigma leads to the ostracization of ex-combatants and their families and weakens their social and community support networks. Ex-combatants facing multiple forms of vulnerabilities—such as disability, poor education, lack of a social network and unemployment—are at the highest risk.

It is worth noting here that the range of social vulnerabilities identified during the field assessments were found to be highest among those populations directly affected by the war, both in terms of exposure to traumatic events, or through displacement. The majority of the directly affected populations are Sri Lankan Tamils, followed by Muslims, and then by the Sinhalese. This creates the potential for persistent horizontal inequalities, which may exacerbate preexisting ethnic tensions, thereby undermining sustainable peace. The field assessments did not find significantly high levels of resentment along the lines of these horizontal inequalities, but global experiences have shown that these are easily exploited for the purposes of conflict and violence.

CONCLUSION

As the Northern and Eastern provinces emerge from a protracted subnational conflict, it will be important to address social issues, including gender vulnerabilities and youth inclusion. Field-level assessments found evidence of persistent psychosocial needs among the war affected populations, alongside pervasive symptoms of trauma, including alcoholism and suicide. Gender-based violence is an issue among the war affected populations, and there is potential for the intergenerational transmission of violence. Current patterns of horizontal inequalities, while not inherently dangerous, have the potential to be exploited for the purposes of undermining sustainable peace. Efforts to promote sustainable peace will necessitate a focus on inclusion and trust within local populations.

NOTES

1. *Horizontal inequalities* are differences in access and opportunities across culturally-defined (or constructed) groups, based on identities such as ethnicity, region, and religion. See Ostby 2008; Cederman, Gleditsch, and Buhaug 2013; United Nations and World Bank 2018.
2. This was not called divorce, as no legal marriage had been undertaken.
3. Most Tamil women were focused specifically on marriage within their ethnic group, as any relationship outside one's own ethnicity is seen as a broader cultural and existential threat to the conventional patriarchal and puritanical expectation of women as bearers of pure and uncontaminated Tamil culture (see Herath 2018).
4. Background paper on Community Institutions.
5. Figures provided by the Ministry of Resettlement, Government of Sri Lanka.
6. Including reports that most loan documents are in Sinhala and not translated into Tamil.
7. Analysis of the Household Income Expenditure Survey (HIES) 2012/13 did find that households in the Northern and Eastern provinces had a higher share of debt versus household consumption, and that most of this debt tended to be informal (see Newhouse and Silwal 2018).
8. For example, the psychiatric clinics of the Mannar District Hospital report that the total number of suicides spiked around 2014, coinciding with resettlement of communities. The inability to cope with the stressors placed on communities during the resettlement process, which was often tied to the fact that there were deficiencies with the provision of basic facilities such as livelihood support and educational support, was cited for this (see Thowfeek 2018).
9. The national suicide rate (crude rate) for Sri Lanka in 2011, was 18.3 (per 100,000 persons), whereas, in the districts of Mullaitivu, Killinochchi, Jaffna, and Batticaloa, the rate was significantly higher, at 28.2, 27.3, 24.5, and 23.7, respectively.
10. The literature on suicide identifies three main factors that lead to suicide namely *burdensomeness*; a feeling that one is a burden to those around them exemplified by their inability to fulfil their social roles; *thwarted belongingness*, an inability to form and maintain intimate relationships; and *the acquired capability for suicide*; a desensitization to fear and pain inducing stimuli, such as violent and aggressive stimuli. See Bryan et al. 2010.

11. At the time of writing, the national-level health statistics (DHS) were not available to corroborate these findings, but data provided by the 2015 Health Bulletin (published by the Ministry of Health, based on an island-wide representative survey conducted by the Department of Census and Statistics) show that districts in the Northern and Eastern provinces had higher alcohol consumption rates than Sri Lanka's average, and these estimates excluded illicit alcohol use (Ministry of Health and Indigenous Medicine 2015).

12. Women noted, however, that if jobs were located too far away from home, and it was difficult to get back in time to take care of domestic duties, the incidence of violence could also increase.

REFERENCES

Aldrich, D. P. 2012. "Social Capital in Post Disaster Recovery: Towards a Resilient and Compassionate East Asian Community." In *Economic and Welfare Impacts of Disasters in East Asia and Policy Responses*, edited by Y. Sawada and S. Oum, 157–78. ERIA Research Project Report 2011-8. Jakarta: ERIA.

Bryan, C. T., K. C. Cukrowicz, C. L. West, and C. E. Marrow. 2010. "Emotional Responses to Trauma." *Journal of Clinical Psychology*, 66 (10): 1044–1956.

Catani, C., N. Jacob, E. Schauer, M. Kohila, and F. Neuner. 2008. "Family Violence, War, and Natural Disasters: A Study of the Effect of Extreme Stress on Children's Mental Health in Sri Lanka." *BMC Psychiatry* 8: 33. https://www.ncbi.nlm.nih.gov/pmc/articles/PMC2386780/.

Cederman, L. E., K. S. Gleditsch, and H. Buhaug. 2013. *Inequality, Grievances, and Civil War*. New York: Cambridge University Press.

de Mel, N., and R. Venugopal. 2016. *Peacebuilding Context Assessment: Sri Lanka 2016*. United Nations Sri Lanka, Colombo.

Department of Census and Statistics. n.d. "Census of Population and Housing 1981." Government of Sri Lanka.

——. n.d. "Census of Population and Housing 2011." Government of Sri Lanka.

Gunasekara, V., M. Philips, K. Romeshun, and M. Munas. 2016. "'Life and Debt': Assessing the Impacts of Participatory Housing Reconstruction in Post-Conflict Sri Lanka." *Stability: International Journal of Security and Development*. 5 (1): 10.

Gunatilaka, R., M. Mayer, and M. Vodopivec. eds. 2010. *The Challenge of Youth Employment in Sri Lanka*. Washington, DC: World Bank.

Herath, D. 2018. "Breakup of Community Social Structures in the War Affected Northern and Eastern Provinces in Sri Lanka." Background Paper No. 3 for the World Bank Socio-Economic Assessment of the Northern and Eastern Provinces, International Centre for Ethnic Studies, Colombo, Sri Lanka.

Jayasuriya, D., R. Jayasuriya, A. Kuowei Tay, and D. Silove. 2016. "Associations of Mental Distress with Residency in Conflict Zones, Ethnic Minority Status, and Potentially Modifiable Social Factors Following Conflict in Sri Lanka: A Nationwide Cross-Sectional Study." *The Lancet: Psychiatry*. February; 3 (2): 145–53.

Justino, P. 2017. "Governance Interventions in Fragile and Conflict-Affected Countries." IDS Working Paper 496, University of Sussex Institute of Development Studies, Sussex, England.

Ministry of Health and Indigenous Medicine. 2015. *Annual Health Bulletin*, 2015. Government of Sri Lanka.

Newhouse, David Locke, Ani Rudra Silwal. 2018. "The State of Jobs in Post-conflict Areas of Sri Lanka (English)." Policy Research Working Paper 8355. World Bank, Washington, DC. http://documents.worldbank.org/curated/en/443541519651773814/The-state-of-jobs-in-post-conflict-areas-of-Sri-Lanka.

Ostby, G. 2008. "Polarization, Horizontal Inequalities and Violent Civil Conflict" *Journal of Peace Research*, 45 (2): 143–162.

Ostby, G., and H. Urdal. 2011. "Education and Civil Conflict: A Review of the Quantitative, Empirical Literature." Background paper prepared for the Education for All Global Monitoring Report 2011, UNESCO, Paris, France.

Sathiadas, M.G., A. Viswalingam, and K. Vijayaratnam. 2018. "Child Abuse and Neglect in the Jaffna District of Sri Lanka—a Study on Knowledge Attitude Practices and Behavior of Health Care Professionals," *BMC Pediatrics* 2018, 18:152.

Somasundaram, D. and S. Sivayokan. 2013. "Rebuilding Community Resilience in a Post-War Context: Developing Insight and Recommendations—A Qualitative Study in Northern Sri Lanka." *International Journal of Mental Health Systems* 73.

Sri Lanka, Northern Province, Jaffna District. 2012. *Study on Gender Based Violence in Jaffna District*, Government of Sri Lanka.

Thowfeek, R. 2018. "Psychosocial Assessment of the War Affected Northern and Eastern Provinces of Sri Lanka: Distress and Growth Post-War." Background Paper 4, World Bank Socio-Economic Assessment of the Northern and Eastern Provinces of Sri Lanka, International Centre for Ethnic Studies, Colombo.

United Nations and World Bank. 2018. *Pathways for Peace: Inclusive Approaches to Preventing Violent Conflict*. Washington, DC: World Bank.

Vincius, J., T. Florencio, L. Grillo, M. do Carmo, P. Franco, P. Martins, A. P. Clemente, C. Santos, M. Vieira, and A. Sawaya. 2011. "Long-Lasting Effects of Undernutrition." *International Journal of Environmental Research and Public Health* 8 (6): 1817–46.

World Bank. 2011. *Conflict, Security and Development: World Development Report 2011*. Washington, DC: World Bank.

———. 2012. *Gender Equality and Development: World Development Report 2012*, Washington, DC: World Bank.

6 The Way Forward
PRIORITIES AND CHALLENGES

Almost a decade has passed since the end of Sri Lanka's civil war, and there is visible growth and convergence between the Northern and Eastern provinces and the rest of the country. However, as the previous sections have shown, several economic challenges and social issues persist. In particular, patterns of pockets of deprivation (e.g., Mullativu, Mannar, and Batticaloa districts), along with horizontal inequalities, create a current set of development challenges that could undermine sustainable peace. This, combined with challenges for youth, are particularly worrying for postconflict development prospects.

POSTCONFLICT DEVELOPMENT: GLOBAL PERSPECTIVES

Global experiences (World Bank 2011; Parks, Collette, and Oppenheim 2013) suggest that restoring confidence and transforming institutions are two key pathways to promoting peace. Measures to restore confidence can vary, but are focused on rebuilding trust between groups of citizens that have been divided by war. Transforming institutions serves to change the incentives, interests and behaviors for violence and war, and can include introducing new "rules of the game" for formal and informal institutions. Both of these measures are self-reinforcing, and create a cyclical pathway toward sustainable peace. This pathway is not linear, and is strongly dependent on context to arrive at local relevant solutions and negotiated actions. Yet, global experiences also indicate that not engaging in these two pathways can increase the probability that violence will once again erupt, and that conflicts will continue. Five global lessons emerge from addressing conflict (World Bank 2011), security, and development challenges:

1. **Community development programs:** First, programs in insecure areas should look to support bottom up state-society relations that focus on a range of outcomes around violence prevention, employment and associated service delivery. Community development programs are one of the most established instruments for postconflict development. One of the largest global examples of a community development program in a postwar context is the National

Community Empowerment Program (PNPM) in Aceh, Indonesia. Launched in 2006, the program sought to bring together all community driven, poverty-related initiatives in Indonesia by providing grants and technical support to poor communities, in order to improve basic infrastructure and social services. The program is one of the largest community-driven development programs in the world, and findings have shown service delivery to be cost effective and aligned with community needs. Similar programs in Liberia, the Philippines, Afghanistan, and the Democratic Republic of Congo have also shown a positive impact on economic outcomes and service delivery. In some cases, and depending on how the program was designed, such programs can also contribute to social cohesion (e.g., Liberia, the Philippines).

2. **Institutional transformation:** Second, these interventions should be complemented with programs for institutional transformation. In Sri Lanka's case, the most relevant examples for institutional transformation draw on experiences with subnational conflicts.[1] Lessons from subnational conflicts highlight the uneven relationship between state institutions and conflict areas, creating a greater need for the political, social and economic inclusion of affected populations. The fact that subnational conflicts are also, on average, of a longer duration, makes addressing the underlying grievances and institutional arrangements all the more pressing to ensure sustainable peace (Parks, Collette, and Oppenheim 2013). Experiences from Aceh, Indonesia, Mindanao, the Philippines, and Southern Thailand can thus be illuminating for Sri Lanka. During the transition period in Aceh, institutional transformation focused on building and maintaining the confidence of both groups involved in the conflict, as well as strengthening institutions to mediate between the center and the periphery. This was followed by a period of institutional transformation at the local level to mediate inter-elite competition and consolidate peace. In Mindanao, the Philippines, programs focused on deepening confidence in the political transition, and on supporting local institutions to mediate local conflicts and promote convergence in development levels. Finally, in Southern Thailand, programs focused on supporting incremental transformation through opening space for peace dialogues and key improvements in policy and governance (Parks, Collette, and Oppenheim 2013). These examples demonstrate the unique features of subnational conflicts, whereby strong national institutions must play a role in promoting inclusion and peace in areas that were formerly at war. Transforming these institutions is a continuous and long term process, often best done through smaller steps at first, followed by larger and more ambitious targets.

3. **Job creation:** Third, "back to basics" job creation programs can help to jumpstart local economic development. These can include simplifying regulations for the private sector, addressing infrastructure bottlenecks, and addressing constraints to accessing finance and investments, in order to bring producers and markets together. An early emphasis on the simplification of business regulations has proven effective; in Bosnia and Herzegovina, for example, the so-called "bulldozer initiative" introduced around 50 reforms aimed at improving the investment climate. Rwanda saw its business registrations grow 10 percent a year by revamping its contract enforcement regime (World Bank 2011).

In many postwar contexts, youth are at greater risk, because of exposure to trauma, participation in armed conflict, or disruptions to their education.

In Kosovo, a program focused on demobilized young combatants and at-risk-youth introduced employment and training programs that included cost-sharing measures with private enterprises. This reduced the social stigma among such youth and successfully ensured employment for a socially excluded category of the population. Evidence from Bosnia and Herzegovina also suggests that individuals suffering from PTSD earned lower wages and were more likely to remain unemployed. Programs that pair psychosocial support and counseling services alongside livelihood and work programs have been used across several countries experiencing conflict, including Cambodia and Uganda (World Bank 2011). Evidence from longitudinal studies indicates greater resilience to mental health problems among those who were working. Finally, cash for work programs are often used in postwar settings to stimulate local economic development and job creation, including in Sri Lanka. Cash for work schemes have been used to restore livelihoods in countries like the Republic of Yemen, Nepal, Afghanistan, Mozambique and Sierra Leone, with secondary objectives of smoothing consumption or alleviating poverty. These programs are typically deployed immediately postwar, although in Afghanistan, there are calls to institutionalize these into a longer term social protection strategy (World Bank 2011).

4. **Women's economic empowerment.** Fourth, involving women in economic empowerment programs is critical for addressing inequitable gender roles. In Nepal, years of civil conflict and interethnic and political violence disproportionately impacted women. Traditional social and economic networks were affected, many women became heads of households, and trafficking and other issues emerged. A large-scale Women's Empowerment Program provided cost-effective training and support to women's groups, promoting literacy and entrepreneurship, and supporting independent sources of incomes. Afghanistan's National Solidarity Program introduced a more balanced gender mix in community organizations, leading to progress in women's leadership.

5. **Access to justice and reconciliation.** Promoting access to justice and reconciliation are key measures for restoring confidence. This includes promoting citizen security, enhancing accountability and citizen oversight, and ensuring good governance, as well as other measures that are credible for supporting reconciliation. Within many postconflict contexts, access to justice can be an important factor in recognizing citizenship and the benefits associated with state programs. Addressing disputes, particularly over issues such as land, can be important, and some countries, for example Kenya and Mali, used combinations of traditional and state institutions to expand access to justice. Justice is also associated with ensuring citizens' equitable access to state resources, and measures to promote transparency and accountability in countries such as Georgia helped to support this transition. Finally, reconciliation processes vary in each country and must be derived from local contexts in order to build inclusive coalitions that lead to credible steps toward peace.

The global experiences described above provide useful lessons for Sri Lanka. However, supporting sustainable peace in the country will also necessitate the careful consideration of emerging lessons from this analysis, as well as the local context, in order to ensure negotiated solutions that work for all stakeholders.

PROMOTING SUSTAINABLE PEACE IN THE NORTHERN AND EASTERN PROVINCES

For the Northern and Eastern provinces, continued efforts at reconciliation, coupled with a focus on job creation, rebuilding local institutions, and restoring confidence and trust will be critical for sustaining peace. Evidence from the field research pointed to these three areas as priority areas for interventions to support local populations. These areas are also well-aligned with global experiences from fragile and conflict affected areas, as well as from countries that have experienced subnational conflict, that focus on restoring confidence and transforming institutions as two key pathways to promoting peace.

The following three areas were identified during the course of this assessment as key areas for attention, in order to best move Sri Lanka toward sustainable peace:

1. **Focus on jobs.** While relief operations in the Northern and Eastern provinces focused on stabilizing livelihoods and promoting local employment, there is a need now to look beyond livelihood development and toward promoting more and better jobs. Employment is not only important for improving household income status, and thereby reducing poverty, but employment was also cited as a pathway to deal with several social issues, including psychosocial challenges. A particular focus on reducing barriers to accessing employment opportunities for women and youth is also important. Female labor force participation is extremely low, and intra-household bargaining power is affected by a relatively larger share of women in the population, leading to the risk of increased exposure to violence. Women face a complex set of barriers to labor force participation, among them cultural and social norms, poor transportation linkages, and a lack of available jobs. A focus on reducing these specific barriers, perhaps by supporting more self-employment opportunities for women, and improving strategic networks and services to reduce mobility challenges, could support increased female labor force participation.

   Maximizing employment creation will necessitate a comprehensive set of interventions designed to support job growth. These include addressing the skills mismatch, providing access to business development and microfinance services, and developing market linkages. This will require strategic investments in infrastructure to unlock market potential, and to support emerging industries and enterprises. Interventions to promote the local business environment through regulatory and legislative incentives will help to address sustainable employment. Finally, with a focus on economic sectors and comparative advantages based on local endowments, this transition will serve micro, small and medium sized enterprises, as well as formal and informal sector workers (Stewart 2015).

   Current endowments would favor promoting and expanding competitiveness in the agriculture sector in the Northern and Eastern provinces. Although the agriculture sector's contributions to the provincial economies are declining, the sector (including farming, livestock and fishing) is the primary source of livelihoods for around 65 percent of the population, and employs 30 percent of the workforce. There is an urgent need to transform the sector from subsistence level production to a commercial-level production system, for improved incomes. Interventions to promote growth in the agriculture sector could focus on improving value chain investments in storage facilities, irrigation systems, and transportation linkages, in order to improve market access. Access to credit for expanding production, such as for multi-use day boats for fishermen, alongside continued technical assistance and extension services for farmers and fishermen, could support the expansion of these sectors. Improving access to information about unpredictable weather patterns and climate change could also prove beneficial.

Identifying possible means for job growth will also involve consideration of the specific constraints faced by women and youth in the Northern and Eastern provinces, many of whom will not favor the agriculture sector for decent work conditions. Addressing barriers to female labor force participation, such as inadequate transportation linkages, gender discrimination in wages, restrictive cultural norms, and the need for child care, alongside skills training, could facilitate greater female labor force participation in specific industries. Promoting access to business development and microfinance services could also help to jumpstart home based businesses for women.

Youth unemployment also remains a challenge, with many young people waiting to take advantage of employment opportunities that are commensurate with their aspirations. Language and labor mobility are challenges for the younger generation, and a focus on English language skills could help to address those issues. In addition, a focus on jobs could look to emerging sectors in the local economy that are in line with local comparative advantages, in order to provide opportunities that are better aligned with job aspirations. In the Eastern Province, potential employment in the tourism sector would necessitate investments in skills and awareness to fill a growing number of jobs in the sector. In the Northern Province, potential in the IT Sector, due to Sri Lanka's position as a global Business Process Outsourcing (BPO) provider, could help to link youth with digital jobs. ICT is also an emerging sector for young women, with vocational training programs in place to train local youth in relevant skills (Asian Development Bank, Deutsche Gesellschaft fuer Internationale Zusammenarbeit 2015).

2. **Support social cohesion and inclusion, particularly for vulnerable populations, to ensure a pathway to sustainable peace.** Nearly a decade after the end of Sri Lanka's civil war, the Northern and Eastern provinces continue to present a complex and interrelated set of socioeconomic vulnerabilities. While there has been convergence along measures of economic growth and infrastructure development, the persistent social issues—especially among the war affected populations—are creating pockets of deprivation and horizontal inequalities. Addressing these needs can focus on the broad based challenges around the increasing gender vulnerabilities identified in this report, women's empowerment, and on the specific services required for war affected populations. Evidence from small-scale programs also demonstrates the need for broader community involvement in effectively addressing social needs and issues.

Addressing the growing set of gender vulnerabilities in the Northern and Eastern provinces will require a cross-cutting approach to ensure that gender is integrated throughout programs and projects in the region. A specific focus on developing leadership among women and promoting women's economic empowerment can begin to address entrenched social and cultural norms. Ensuring adequate support services for victims of gender-based violence, including state and nonstate supported solutions, can also help to address key vulnerabilities.

Alongside programs to promote livelihoods and incomes, specific services designed to address the needs of war affected populations can focus on raising awareness to reduce social stigma. Supporting recently resettled IDPs and other affected populations in restoring assets and expanding home based production will also unlock potential assets for development, which will thus contribute to local economic growth. Ensuring adequate counseling and other support services will be essential for the continued reduction of vulnerabilities. Engaging nonstate actors to support the extension of these services could also assist in tracking the status and needs of these services. Finally, continued follow up assessments, to understand the impacts of interventions and programs on the reduction of vulnerabilities, will be critical.

Broader support for local economic development could use an approach that leverages participatory planning and methods of community level development that also serve to address community-level vulnerabilities. Global experiences show that broader social issues, such as collective trauma, alcoholism and suicide, can often be effectively dealt with at a community level. Community mobilization and empowerment can also help to restore support structures that have been damaged by the conflict.

Taken together, these interventions can provide a strong social support system for vulnerable populations in the Northern and Eastern provinces that are still negatively affected by the war. Addressing these needs will reduce the emerging horizontal inequalities and ensure pathways to sustainable peace.

3. **Restore accountability and trust through governance and participation.**
Addressing the multi-faceted impacts of war requires a multi-dimensional process toward postconflict development. To date, much of the emphasis in Sri Lanka has been on the rebuilding and reconstruction of physical infrastructure, economic recovery and, to a certain extent, broader reconciliation efforts. These are in line with typical postwar recovery efforts, with much of the immediate postwar reconstruction largely state-led in nature (Keerawella 2013). In transitioning to local economic development, there will need to be more room for development at the grassroots level, targeted to the economic and social empowerment of people and local communities, as well as the inclusion of other actors and stakeholders. This will foster other dimensions of conflict recovery, including social and economic well-being and governance and participation (Keerawella 2013). While some programs have introduced more participatory planning, more efforts are needed to systematize this.

Addressing these needs effectively will require revisiting the current institutional setup for service delivery and local governance. Sri Lanka's current bifurcated system of service delivery has inherent inefficiencies and dysfunctions, with certain services delivered through national line ministries and field offices, and a second set delivered through locally elected governments. This institutional structure has led to fragmented or overlapping service delivery at the local level, and a lack of adequate planning to address local needs. In addition, with much of the service delivery done through central government bodies, there is little potential for accountability at the local level. Promoting social cohesion is as much about political inclusion as it is about social and economic inclusion, and as suggested by global experiences, lack of participation, voice and accountability are key elements of conflict (Keerawella 2013).

In the short term, strengthening bottom up and participatory planning, combined with improved coordination between different branches of government, could help to address some of these institutional inefficiencies.[2] Participatory planning has already been introduced through several projects in the Northern and Eastern provinces, and could be further institutionalized. In addition, improved coordination between divisional secretaries (DS) and the local authorities (LA) through existing coordination committees could reduce institutional overlap. Secondly, area based planning between the DS and the LA could lead to the identification of strategic investments that will unlock the potential growth and development of a given area. Strengthening citizen engagement and downward accountability would also go a long way to improve inclusion and social cohesion.

In addition, a key step toward restoring trust would be to tackle several land management challenges in the Northern and Eastern provinces. While the debates over land held by the military in high security zones will need to be negotiated within the context of the country, there are several short-term measures that could help to support trust building. First, many people are slowly returning to land that had been abandoned, and they face challenges on a range of issues, including the clearing of land and land disputes. Support to recently resettled and returned populations could be in the form of clearing land, providing access to services and connections to electricity and water, etc. In addition, supporting and expanding programs that have helped to provide access to justice for resolving land disputes between people will be critical for helping local populations to regain access to key assets, as well as to restore confidence. Examples of these programs in Sri Lanka include mobile justice centers and alternative dispute resolution mechanisms. Bolstering such programs will also be key for supporting women to gain access to the essential certifications that will enable them to make use of land assets.

CONCLUSION

Sri Lanka's Northern and Eastern provinces are transitioning from a period of postwar recovery to local economic development. This will require a better understanding of local endowments and interventions that will unlock the potential growth and development of sustainable employment opportunities. Recently resettled and returned populations will benefit from assistance in the form of clearing land and access to services. For the broader population, a focus on jobs would need to address barriers to female labor force participation, as well as the mismatch between aspirations and opportunities among local youth; expanding relevant vocational training programs would be an important step toward addressing this mismatch. Such efforts should be complimented by regulatory and legislative incentives that will help promote the local business environment. Continued attention to social vulnerabilities is also needed to address horizontal inequalities and ensure pathways to sustainable peace. Hence, alongside programs to promote livelihoods and incomes, efforts are needed to reduce social stigma for ex-combatants and other groups. Finally, improved local participation, planning and coordination is needed to fully unlock the economic potential of the Northern and Eastern provinces, and to restore accountability and trust.

NOTES

1. Subnational conflicts differ from fragile and conflict-affected states in three important ways: (a) Subnational conflicts tend to span several decades, fluctuating between periods of high intensity and relative calm; (b) Subnational conflicts often take place in states with high capacity and strong national institutions; (c) There is no clear relationship between economic growth and subnational conflict; many national economies experiencing high economic growth have also experienced continued conflict.

2. Examples from the assessment pointed to instances where either social programs were not being received by beneficiaries, where counseling programs did not have qualified staff, or where multiple agencies were implementing programs with similar objectives. Multiple community organizations were established within the same location to promote access to different programs. Institutional coordination is addressed through divisional and district level committees, but they are often weak or ineffective. In addition, no planning with the objective of promoting economic growth, job creation, or addressing social needs is currently undertaken. Such planning, if implemented, could begin to liaise with strengthened community organizations with the objective of promoting area based growth and development through strategic infrastructure investments and coordinated service delivery.

REFERENCES

Asian Development Bank, Deutsche Gesellschaft fuer Internationale Zusammenarbeit. 2015. "Country Gender Assessment Sri Lanka: An Update." ADB and GIZ. https://openaccess .adb.org.

Keerawella, G. 2013. "Post-War Sri Lanka: Is Peace a Hostage of the Military Victory?: Dilemmas of Reconciliation, Ethnic Cohesion, and Peace-Building." International Centre for Ethnic Studies, Colombo, Sri Lanka.

Parks, T., N. Colleta, and B. Oppenheim. 2013. *The Contested Corners of Asia: Subnational Conflict and International Development Assistance.* San Francisco: Asia Foundation.

Stewart, Frances. 2015. "Employment in Conflict and Post-Conflict Situations." UNDP Human Development Report Office. New York.

World Bank. 2011. *Conflict, Security and Development: World Development Report 2011.* Washington, DC: World Bank.

——. 2012. *Gender Equality and Development: World Development Report 2012*, Washington, DC: World Bank.